STUDIES IN ROMANCE LANGUAGES: 43

John E. Keller, Editor

The Presence of Pessoa

English, American,
and Southern African
Literary Responses

GEORGE MONTEIRO

THE UNIVERSITY PRESS OF KENTUCKY

Publication of this volume was made possible in part by grants from the Calouste Gulbenkian Foundation, Lisbon; Luso-American Development Foundation; and the National Endowment for the Humanities.

Scholarly publisher for the Commonwealth,
serving Bellarmine College, Berea College, Centre
College of Kentucky, Eastern Kentucky University,
The Filson Club Historical Society, Georgetown College,
Kentucky Historical Society, Kentucky State University,
Morehead State University, Murray State University,
Northern Kentucky University, Transylvania University,
University of Kentucky, University of Louisville,
and Western Kentucky University.

Editorial and Sales Offices: The University Press of Kentucky
663 South Limestone Street, Lexington, Kentucky 40508-4008

98 99 00 01 02   5 4 3 2 1

Frontispiece: Portrait of Fernando Pessoa by Júlio Pomar,
courtesy of the Calouste Gulbenkian Foundation.

Library of Congress Cataloging-in-Publication Data

Monteiro, George.
    The presence of Pessoa : English, American, and Southern African literary responses / George Monteiro.
        p.   cm.—(Studies in Romance languages ; 43)
    Includes bibliographical references and index.
    ISBN 0-8131-2053-5 (cloth : alk. paper)
    1. English literature—Portuguese influences. 2. Pessoa,
Fernando, 1888-1935—Influence. 3. American literature—Portuguese influences. 4. Southern African literature—Portuguese influences.
5. Pessoa, Fernando, 1888-1935—Appreciation—Great Britain.
6. Pessoa, Fernando, 1888-1935—Apprciation—United States.
7. Pessoa, Fernando, 1888-1935—Appreciation—Africa, Southern.
8. English literature—20th century—History and criticism.
9. American literature—20th century,—History and criticism.
10. Southern African literature—History and criticism.   I. Title.
II. Series: Studies in Romance languages (Lexington, Ky.) ; 43.
PR129.P67M66   1998
820.9'0091—dc21   97-40435

To Brenda

Contents

Illustrations

Preface

A writer can do no more than surmise what posterity will do with his work. Fernando Pessoa, thinking himself through the natural principles of posthumous literary reputation, reached the conclusion that poets won lasting fame not for the corpus of their work but for the handful of poems that would survive in the public memory and on which a literary reputation might be based. Though he liked much in Shakespeare, for instance, Ariel's song from *The Tempest* became his Arnoldian touchstone for the whole of Shakespeare. That song alone, he ventured to say, proved that Shakespeare was a greater poet than, for instance, Tennyson.

It is sometimes proposed that writers create canons, traditions, and lasting literary reputations by their choice of works to read, praise, rewrite, and incorporate. If so, we don't need to worry much about Pessoa's future literary fame. The English-language poets considered here are part of a larger chorus that includes the voices of Carlos Drummond de Andrade (Brazilian Portuguese), Antonio Tabucchi (Italian), Angel Crespo (Spanish), and Paul Celan (German), to name just a few.

The Presence of Pessoa considers some of the English-language poets who have put Pessoa to their own uses. Its nets have been cast wide among writers to use as examples, though there has been no attempt to be exhaustive as to poets or as to individual canons of work. It focuses mainly on specific literary uses, which themselves might be seen as indicating possible touchstones in Pessoa's own vast opus. Examples include Thomas Merton's decision to work with only the Zen-like poems of one of Pessoa's poetry-writing selves, Lawrence Ferlinghetti's rewriting of Pessoa's single fictional text on the unholy marriage of capitalism and anarchism, Allen Ginsberg's

redirection of Pessoa's boisterous and irreverent tribute to Walt
Whitman against a Pessoa he calls "Pessoa Schmessoa." In
some instances there is evidence indicating that Pessoa's influence extends well beyond a single text or two, as will be seen in
the discussions of Edwin Honig and Charles Eglington. In one
instance—that of Joyce Carol Oates—one can build only a
largely circumstantial case, since the writer herself has not acknowledged Pessoa's influence.

This book incorporates material previously published in *Portuguese Studies, Revista da Faculdade de Letras,* and *Tabacaria,* which
appears here with permission. Unpublished material by Roy Campbell is quoted with the consent of the University of Texas at Austin
and the permission of Ad. Donker (Pty) Ltd. and Francisco Campbell
Custódio. The latter two also granted permission to reprint Campbell: "Rounding the Cape." Mécia de Sena has permitted quotation
from Jorge de Sena's letters to Edith Sitwell. Edwin Honig granted
permission to reproduce his "Being Someone" and "Pessoa's Last
Masquer-ade," and Dennis Silk allowed me to reproduce his
"Mandive House" and "Under the Weather." Edouard Roditi's "The
Warning" and "Auto Psychoanalysis" are reprinted courtesy of Jon
Cone from *World Letter* (Iowa City, Iowa). Allen Ginsberg's
"Salutations to Fernando Pessoa" (from *Cosmopolitan Greetings:
Poems, 1986-1994,* © 1988) and "I Love Old Whitman So" (from
White Shroud: Poems, 1980-1985, © 1986) are reprinted by permis-
sion of HarperCollins Publishers. Selections from *The Collected
Poems of Thomas Merton* (© 1968 by The Abbey of Gethsemani) are
reproduced by permission of New Directions Publishing. Michael
Hamburger's "Lisbon Night," from *Collected Poems, 1941-1994,* is re-
produced by permission of *Anvil* Press Poetry Ltd.

Júlio Pomar's portrait of Fernando Pessoa is in the collection of
the Centro de Arte Moderna José de Azeredo Perdigão (Fundação
Calouste Gulbenkian, Lisbon) and is used with permission.

The American Philosophical Society and the Calouste Gulbenkian Foundation generously supported my research at the
Biblioteca Nacional in Lisbon at the right time.

I thank my colleagues at Brown University who make the
Department of Portuguese and Brazilian Studies a congenial
place for work and study. Of the many individuals I am indebted to, I shall single out only three by name: José Blanco,
who has always been willing to share his vast knowledge of

Pessoa's life and all things Pessoan, Onésimo Teotónio Almeida, for his support and generosity over the years, and David H. Hirsch, for his exemplary scholarship.

Brenda Murphy's suggestions have proved invaluable—once again.

1

Works and Days

Fernando Pessoa (1888-1935) is the last great discovery in twentieth-century Western poetry. Only now is he being accorded his rightful high place among the great poets of the twentieth century by readers and critics of the English-speaking world. Belatedly following the example of translators and readers in France and Germany, Spain, and the Netherlands, even the famous Anglo-American critics Harold Bloom and George Steiner have discovered him.[1] Spot drawings in the *New Yorker* (the work of Belgian artist Benoit van Innis) place Pessoa's poetry squarely within the pantheon of modern Western poetry alongside the work of the Austrian Rainer Maria Rilke and the Anglo-American T.S. Eliot.[2]

But if Anglo-American critics and scholars have been slow to read and appreciate Pessoa, poets have not. For their own purposes and according to their lights, poets on both sides of the Atlantic began discovering Pessoa's writings in the 1950s. From Edouard Roditi and Thomas Merton to John Wain, from Lawrence Ferlinghetti to Allen Ginsberg, and from Edwin Honig to Roy Campbell, each of these poets has found a way to incorporate an essential aspect of Pessoa in his own work. That different poets have seen different things in the writing they admire is to be expected, but Pessoa's canon offers an extraordinary feast for poets on the lookout for ideas, themes, and images. His poetry has suited the antipoetry agenda of Thomas Merton as readily as his fiction has confirmed the willful anarchist dreams of Lawrence Ferlinghetti. And then there is the odd case of Joyce Carol Oates, who disclaimed all knowledge of Portugal and its culture while setting down Portuguese stories and parables dictated to her by one "Fernandes."

Perhaps no other poet of his time can be said to surpass Pessoa in creative versatility. Truly he is sui generis, if only in the number and variety of poets he consciously brought into being. He became the progenitor of fictional poets who themselves became, ingeniously, the creator of scores of real poems. Other poets have written poetry in the voices of fictional, historical, and literary figures—one thinks of the English Robert Browning, the Argentine Jorge Luis Borges, and the Danish Søren Kierkegaard—but Pessoa is unique in writing for each of the major figures he created (his "heteronyms") a body of poetry that not only is readily identifiable as the singular work of its putatively fictional author but also in itself constitutes an invaluable contribution to Portuguese, European, and world poetry. No poet was ever blessed with a more appropriate family name, for *Pessoa* means both person and persona, an opportunity that the poet seems to have recognized at an early age, for the writer who became, some would argue, Portugal's greatest poet (with the notable exception, perhaps, of the sixteenth-century Luís de Camões) took to addressing letters to himself at the age of five or six. He attributed these letters to an imaginary companion he identified as 'Le Chevalier de Pas.' In time this French companion was followed by other imaginary selves, themselves destined to divide and subdivide into a veritable legion of such projected figures of the imagination. Pessoa's suggestive name offered him an unmatchable creative opportunity that he seems to have taken as a challenge. At last look—"last look" because new ones keep turning up—the count stood at seventy-two such dramatis personae in what Pessoa called his "intimate theatre of the self." True, some were merely names or little more, but several were full-blown figures.

The poet was born Fernando António Nogueira Pessoa in Lisbon in 1888. The day was June 13, the birthday, as it happened, of Santo António, the city's patron—hence the source of the future poet's middle name. Pessoa received his formal education in southern Africa, and because at the time much of this geographical area was under British rule, his education was thoroughly English. At seven he arrived in Durban, the capital of the British colony of Natal, in the company of his mother, who, after the death of his father, had remarried. His stepfather was the new consul in Durban. Pessoa remained in Natal—except for a rare visit to Portugal—until, at seventeen, he returned to Lisbon, expecting to continue his studies at the university. He matriculated, but within weeks a student strike interrupted classes. The strike was over soon enough, but the young Pessoa decided not to return to the university. Instead, he took up what would become a lifelong job, with the exception of brief stints at running a printing house and at publishing: handling the foreign-language correspondence of business firms in Lisbon's commercial district. The cofounder and coeditor of *Orpheu* and *Athena*, he contributed numerous essays and poems to newspapers and literary journals. Writing both in Portuguese and English, he worked in all the major genres (drama, fiction, essay, translation, poetry) and contributed to several disciplines (including philosophy, sociology, business, and commerce). In 1934 he published a poetic sequence entitled *Mensagem*, the one book in Portuguese that appeared during his lifetime. Although he published much of his work under his own name, some of his strongest poetry he attributed to his three major heteronyms—Alberto Caeiro, Ricardo Reis, and Álvaro de Campos. *Livro do Desassossego* (*The Book of Disquiet*), a collection of aperçus, thoughts, and meditations, first published in 1982, he credited to one Bernardo Soares, a semiheteronym. Pessoa died in Lisbon on November 30, 1935.

Since he spent his formative years in a city that was culturally British, Pessoa was bilingual. Most of his first poems, in fact, were composed in English. Only after returning definitively to Lisbon in 1905 did he turn to composing principally in Portuguese. Not surprisingly, he ultimately did his best work in his native tongue. He wrote a good deal of poetry over his own name (his so-called orthonymic poems), but much of his best work he attributed to his heteronyms—Caeiro, Reis, Campos. During the last year of his life he answered the critic Adolfo Casais Monteiro's question regarding the genesis of his three great heteronyms:

One day it occurred to me to pull a prank on [Mário] Sá-Carneiro—to invent a bucolic poet, of a complicated sort, and to present him—I no longer remember how—in some sort of realistic way. I spent a few days fleshing out this poet but I got nowhere. Then, when I had finally given up—it was on March 8, 1914—I found myself before a tall chest

1. Heteronym: Alberto Caeiro by José de Almada Negreiros. Façade engraving, Faculdade de Letras, Universidade de Lisboa.

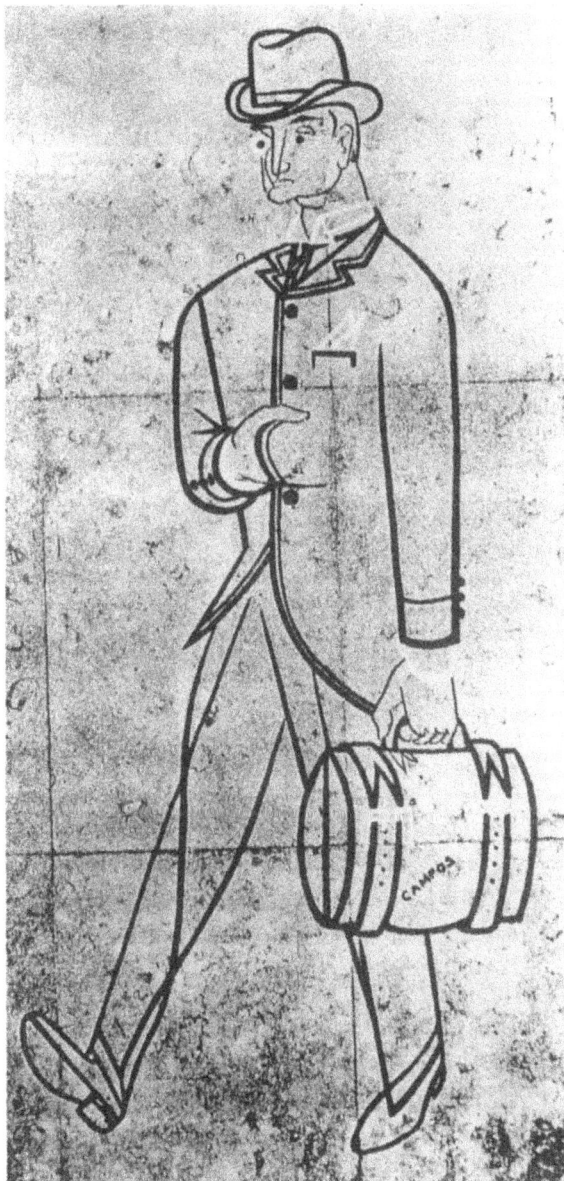

2. Heteronym: Álvaro de Campos by José de Almada
Negreiros. Façade engraving, Faculdade de Letras,
Universidade de Lisboa.

3. Heteronym: Ricardo Reis by
José de Almada Negreiros. Fa-
çade engraving, Faculdade de
Letras, Universidade de Lisboa.

of drawers, took up a piece of paper and began to write, remaining up-right all the while since I always stand when I can. I wrote thirty some poems in a row, all in a kind of ecstasy, the nature of which I shall never fathom. It was the triumphant day of my life, and I shall never have another like it. I began with a title, *The Keeper of Sheep* ["O guardador de rebanhos"]. And what followed was the appearance of someone within me to whom I promptly assigned the name of Alberto Caeiro. Please excuse the absurdity of what I am about to say, but there had appeared within me, then and there, my own master. It was my immediate sensation. So much so that, with those thirty odd poems written, I immediately took up another sheet of paper and wrote as well, in order, the six poems that make up "Oblique Rain" ["Chuva oblíqua"] by Fernando Pessoa. . . . It marked the return from Fernando Pessoa/Alberto Caeiro to Fernando Pessoa alone. Or better still, it was Fernando Pessoa's reaction to his own inexistence as Alberto Caeiro.

With Alberto Caeiro's appearance, I set out right away—instinc-tively and subconsciously—to discover some disciples for him. I sepa-rated out the latent Ricardo Reis from his false paganism, discerned his name, and made adjustments—for at that time I could already see him. And suddenly, deriving in a way opposite to that of Ricardo Reis, there came impetuously to my mind a new individual. In a flash and at the typewriter, without interruption or any emendation, there emerged the "Triumphal Ode" ["Ode triunfal"] by Álvaro de Campos—the ode now known by that title along with the man who bears that name.

I had created, therefore, an inexistent coterie. I fixed everything into plausible patterns. I gauged influences, discovered friendships, and heard, within myself, discussions and disagreements over criteria. In all this the creator of every thing and every one mattered the least, I think. It seemed as if everything had taken place independently of me. And this is still the way things seem to go. If someday I am able to pub-lish Ricardo Reis's discussion with Álvaro de Campos over esthetics, you will see just how different they are and that I am of no matter in the whole thing.[3]

Earlier, in 1928, in an article in the journal *Presença*, whose ed-itors had proclaimed him "Master" among living poets, Pessoa had defined what he meant by "heteronyms": "A pseudonymic work is, except for the name with which it is signed, the work of an author writing as himself; a heteronymic work is by an author writing outside his own personality: it is the work of a complete individuality made up by him, just as the utterances of some character in a drama would be."[4] Some further clarification of the relationship of the heteronyms to the poet who "created" them is available in the truncated beginning piece Pessoa wrote for his never compiled or published collected works: "I divide what I have written into orthonymic and heteronymic work. I do not divide it into autonymic and pseudonymic work because those that I publish under fictitious names do not represent either my opinions or my emotions."[5]

Undoubtedly, Pessoa's heteronyms contributed immensely to the poet's "true" life, which was the interior life of the artist and thinker. What happened to him publicly, in the streets of Lisbon, in the cafés, in the offices of the firms he served as clerk of correspondence, as journal polemicist—political and artistic—or as the quondam lover of a young typist named Ophelia (aptly so, to this writer with a Hamlet complex)—all this pales before the reality of his interior life, lived in a far and distant land, of which his essays, stories and, above all, poems provide news. In fact, so richly complex was this life that no single one of his many identities—and certainly not the one he called Fernando Pessoa himself (*êle mesmo*)—could glean his teeming brain. It took the whole complement of his heteronyms, especially Caeiro, Reis and Campos, to enact that drama-within-persons (*drama em gente*) that he called his life's work. That work and the surprises it always brought him remained to the last his preoccupation and his sustenance.

Since Pessoa's death in 1935, his fame and literary reputation have grown gradually and steadily, first in his native Portugal, of course, but over the last forty years throughout Europe (including the United Kingdom), South America (especially Brazil), and the United States. In England the notorious necromancer Aleister Crowley had known of Pessoa since 1930 or so, less as a poet than as a student of the occult, though, later, he did describe "Don Fernando Pessoa" as "a really good poet, the only man who has ever written Shakespearean Sonnets in the manner of Shakespeare." "It is about the most remarkable literary phenomena in my experience," he marveled.[6] In the first decade or so after Pessoa's death, there appeared English translations of only a few of his poems, the first by Charles Ley in the Portuguese journal *Presença* in November 1938 and two by Leonard S. Downes in an author's edition printed in Lisbon in 1947.

It can be argued that English recognition of Pessoa's original contribution to modern Portuguese poetry started with the appearance, shortly after the end of World War II, of the second edition of the *Oxford Book of Portuguese Verse*. The first edition, published in 1925, was compiled by the English scholar and Lusophile Aubrey F.G. Bell. At that time Pessoa was already well known in Lisbon as a poet, critic, and translator, but Bell's interests did not extend to the moderns, and he excluded Pessoa from his selection.

In 1952 Oxford brought Bell's work up-to-date. The new editor, B. Vidigal, chose 1946 as his cutoff date, "above all for its literary significance, for it saw the publication of the fourth and last volume of the complete poetical works of Fernando Pessoa, which, except for *Mensagem*, had until then been scattered in reviews." Only a few years had elapsed, but already one might attempt, he asserted, "to assess the far-reaching effects of this literary event." Vidigal began by sketching out the story of Pessoa's posthumous reputation, continued with an acknowledgment of his role in calling attention to contemporaries such as Mário de Sá-Carneiro and defining "the real importance of the creative talent of António Nobre, Cesário Verde, Camilo Pessanha, and A. Gomes Leal." In short, Vidigal writes, "[Pessoa] paved the way for the generation of poets now writing, and it is through him that their creed is finding a warmer response among the public."[7]

Pessoa's appearance in the revised Oxford version of Portugal's poetic canon caught the immediate attention of the South African Roy Campbell. He initiated a translation project by characteristically talking up his poets—especially Pessoa—in radio broadcasts. But his plan for a collection of Pessoa in English translation had not yet materialized when, in 1957, he died in a car accident near Setubal, just south of Lisbon. Some of the work he had completed appeared posthumously in *Portugal*, a historical and cultural guide published in 1958. He left unfinished in manuscript a study of Pessoa, under contract to a London publisher, that did not achieve print for nearly four decades. (The surviving draft of this unfinished work appears below in the Appendix.)

In the mid-1950s, in addition to Campbell's work on Pessoa, there was the translation of "O Mostrengo," a poem from *Mensagem,* by the American poet W.S. Merwin. It was read over the BBC at the time but appears not to have been published. And in 1955 there were the lines translated by the polylingual Edouard Roditi for "The Several Names of Fernando Pessoa," his pioneering essay in *Poetry* magazine. Over the next decade, however, versions of Pessoa in English came to a halt. There was nothing until 1966, when Thomas Merton, the American trappist monk, writer, and poet, published translations of twelve poems by Pessoa's antipastoral heteronym Alberto Caeiro. Two years later the poet-editor Stanley Burnshaw included Pessoa's "Autopsicografia" and the poem beginning "Entre o sono e o sonho" in *The Poem Itself,* an innovative critical anthology.[8] The Galician scholar-poet Ernesto Guerra Da Cal, better known as a student of the work of the Portuguese novelist Eça de Queiroz, offered excellent readings of Pessoa's poems, along with literal translations. After three decades and numerous editions, this work remains in print.

The year 1968 also saw the publication of the first of five chapbooks devoted to Pessoa and his principal heteronyms by the Scot J.R. Green. The last in the series appeared in 1975. In 1969 there appeared Michael Hamburger's *The Truth of Poetry: Tensions in Modern Poetry from Baudelaire to the 1960s,* a magisterial study that includes ten excellent pages on Pessoa. Hamburger's talent as poet-translator is evident in lines he translated to argue his case for Pessoa.[9]

For Pessoa in English dress, 1971 was a banner year, bringing the publication of several volumes of translations. Edwin Honig's versions were published by Swallow Press in Chicago, Jonathan Griffin's, in four small volumes, by Carcanet Press of Oxford, and Peter Rickard's by the Edinburgh University Press. Two years later F.E.G. Quintanilha brought out translations of sixty poems under the aegis of the University of Wales Press in Cardiff. In some measure these early translators paved the way for the increasing interest in Pessoa's work marked over the years by translations by, among others, Jean Longland, Suzette Macedo, James Greene and Clara de Azevedo Mafra, Richard

Zenith, and the present writer. Some sort of record for translations of Pessoa was set in 1991 when no fewer than four English translations of *Livro do Desassossego*, that cornucopia of fragments, saw print. Edward Mac Adam's version was brought out by Pantheon Books in New York, Margaret Jull Costa's by Serpent's Tail in London and New York, Richard Zenith's by Carcanet in Manchester, and Iain Watson's by Quartet Books in London.

The Presence of Pessoa takes as its subject several English-language writers whose work has been influenced by their reading of Fernando Pessoa. It is not without significance that most of them have read Pessoa in translation. Thomas Merton first read Octavio Paz's Spanish translations, though he later secured an edition of Pessoa in the original.[10] Lawrence Ferlinghetti read a French translation of *O banqueiro anarquista* (*The Anarchist Banker*), Pessoa's cerebral tale about economics and power. Allen Ginsberg read Edwin Honig's English translations, as did Karl Shapiro. Both Ginsberg and Shapiro have written poems recording the fact. Honig himself, however, first encountered Pessoa's poetry in Portuguese. He heard a Portuguese fisherman recite "Mar português" ("Portuguese Sea"), a lyric from *Mensagem*, in an English bar in the Algarvian town of Praia da Rocha.

The always surprising Joyce Carol Oates offers a special, problematic case. She does not admit to having heard of Fernando Pessoa (let alone having read his poetry) when, in 1975, she published *"The Poisoned Kiss" and Other Stories from the Portuguese*, a collection of intertextually related tales attributed, on the title page, to "Fernandes/Joyce Carol Oates." Hers is a very curious case of pseudonymity that repays consideration within a context of Pessoan aesthetics.

If Oates shares with Pessoa an interest in fictional authorial selves, the other Americans who have taken up Pessoa have done so with particular agendas. Thomas Merton heard in the antiphilosophical philosophical poems of the heteronym Alberto Caeiro the overlaid voices of St. John of the Cross and Zen. Only when Honig heard the resounding echoes of Walt Whitman—barbaric yawp and all—in the heteronymic Álvaro de Campos's boisterous "Maritime Ode" did he feel stirred to make good on his well-intentioned promise to translate Pessoa.

Ginsberg expresses, comically, his anxiety in discovering that Pessoa preceded him in recognizing the radical sexuality and explosive comic energy of Whitman, becoming thereby—preceding Ginsberg by decades—the nineteenth-century American bard's first truly modern disciple. Ginsberg's fellow Beat poet Ferlinghetti, on the other hand, reached out to a different Pessoa, one speaking in the satirical political voice of the armchair anarchist, for his theme, structure, and even armature, in *Love in the Days of Rage*, a novella published in 1988.

Two important South African writers have heard the siren calls of the many-voiced Pessoa. Roy Campbell and Charles Eglington came to Pessoa partly because of his connection during his early years to Durban, though neither of them claims anything less than universality for the Portuguese poet. A great admirer of Portugal—its history, people, and literature—Campbell set forth in the early 1950s to write a book on Pessoa for an Anglo-American audience. Eglington, a poet of considerable reputation in his time, committed suicide before he managed to bring out the book of poems he had promised his readers. To the journal *Contrast 16* (1967), however, he released his "Homage to Fernando Pessoa," a suite of poems deriving from Pessoa's *Mensagem*. Along with his translation of Pessoa's "O Mostrengo," these poems were collected in the posthumous volume *Under the Horizon* (1977).

Other English-language admirers of Pessoa's work include the British novelist-scholar-poet John Wain and his Anglo-Indian student-protégé-colleague Andrew Harvey. In 1979 Wain published "Thinking About Mr. Person," a poetic sequence about Pessoa that addressed, among other matters, Pessoa's "Englishness":

> Mr Person did not need to look for England:
> he carried a little of her inside himself.
> He wrote some poems in English.
> He often had English thoughts.
> He once saw Queen *Victoria*, for God's sake!
> It happened in South Africa,
> when he was at school in Durban.[11]

Andrew Harvey, for his part, has published both translations of Pessoa and a book-length sequence of engaging and amusing poems that center on the relationship of one Fernando to a rather straight-talking woman named Lydia. In all likelihood, this Lydia is based on the ever-silent Lídia so often addressed in polished verse by Pessoa's heteronymic Ricardo Reis. Harvey's jeu d'esprit, published in 1985, is entitled *No Diamonds, No Hat, No Honey.* Over the years various golden opportunities to make Pessoa's work better known in the England-speaking world failed to materialize. During Pessoa's lifetime, for instance, *O banqueiro anarquista* was almost translated into English. In January 1935 the young Adolfo Casais Monteiro offered Pessoa the services of the English poet Richard Aldington for the purpose. Moreover, as Casais Monteiro informed Pessoa, "Aldington is the intimate friend of one of the partners in the firm Chatto & Windus, which usually publishes his work." But Pessoa countered with the information that he planned to translate the work himself and that he knew how to engage an agent who would place it with a London publisher.[12] Pessoa did not live to do his own translation, and fifty-three years elapsed before Pessoa's work appeared in English, as "The Anarchist Banker: A Fiction," in Edwin Honig's translation.

A second opportunity to promote Pessoa in England came to little or nothing after the promising initiative of Jorge de Sena, the Portuguese poet and critic. In March 1953 Sena brought Pessoa's English-language poetry to the attention of the English poet Edith Sitwell. He sent her a copy of *35 Sonnets*, inscribing it to "Doctor Edith Sitwell, / with gratitude, remembering the / kindness of her genius, this / little and precious side of one / of the greatest portuguese poets."[13] Sena's gift evoked from Sitwell words of appreciation to Sena and praise for Pessoa:

> I am most grateful to you for your great kindness in sending me the book, the Sonnets are flawlessly formed. Who translated them? Or were they, actually, written in English? I imagine they were *not*, but they are so flawless as Sonnets, that one can hardly believe they are translations.
>
> They are lucid and lucent,—carved from some transparent stone that is a trap for the light.[14]

Sitwell's carefully selected words pleased Sena, who, hoping that Sitwell would play a major role in bringing Pessoa to the attention of the English literary establishment, replied by return mail with several paragraphs about Pessoa's life, ideas, and poems.

In February 1954, Sena again wrote to Sitwell, partly to say that he had taken the liberty of quoting Sitwell's encomium in a recent piece on Fernando Pessoa and English literature. He had not had time to ask her for her permission to quote from her letter, he explained, but had only said "that Dr. Edith Sitwell had found them [the sonnets] 'translucent.'"[15] "This extraordinary woman," Sena later recalled, "admired the sonnets, recognizing in them an undeniable richness" as well as evidence of the high quality of the poet's vision.[16] But as Sena must have surmised, Sitwell never made public her admiration for Pessoa's poems.[17]

The details of still another opportunity lost to the history of Pessoa's literary reputation in the English-speaking world are recalled by the American poet Hugo Leckey. He tells of a festive evening at the home of Edwin Honig in the mid to late 1960s in honor of the poet Robert Lowell. Lowell was "so deep in his cups that all he could do was demand more," recalls Leckey. "Most of his bodily activities were successfully anesthetized except for his tongue," continues Leckey, "and this he used to tell Edwin that he absolutely had to read an amazing Portuguese poet called Fernando Pessoa." Honig told Lowell that he had been translating Pessoa for years. He would like to show him his manuscript. But Lowell was "oblivious" to Honig's words, and while Honig fetched his manuscript, the drunken Lowell "blathered on" to Leckey "about this amazing poet who wrote in various voices and personas." Leckey quoted some Pessoa to Lowell, hoping to let him know in that way what Honig had been doing by way of translation for some time. "It was to no avail," for when Honig presented his manuscript to Lowell, the latter, "without a glance at the material," "set it down beside his briefcase and said, 'Don't expect to hear from me for at least six months. I have too much to read. Now, Edwin, I want to tell you about this amazing Portuguese poet. Pessoa, Portuguese . . .'"[18] Unfortunately Robert Lowell, like Sitwell, failed to make public his admiration for Fernando Pessoa.

Despite these lost opportunities, Pessoa's cosmopolitan reputation has grown in the past quarter of a century. Consequently, Harold Bloom's praise for Pessoa in *The Western Canon*, welcome though it is, does not surprise us in the way that any published praise by Lowell (or by Lowell's friend, the American poet Elizabeth Bishop, who also knew Pessoa's poetry) might have done thirty years ago. Still, it is important that Bloom included Pessoa as one among a mere twenty-six writers selected for treatment in his provocative and contentious book. No matter that Bloom considers Pessoa, along with Jorge Luis Borges and Pablo Neruda, part of what Bloom calls the "Hispanic-Portuguese Whitman."[19] Much of what Bloom writes about Pessoa and his heteronyms, Alberto Caeiro and Álvaro de Campos, covers ground long familiar to students of Pessoa, but here and there Bloom strikes an original attitude or makes a sharp observation, such as when he distinguishes between García Lorca's Whitman (known to the Spanish poet at second hand) and Pessoa's Whitman (known to the Portuguese poet in the original). Or when he writes, "Pessoa-Campos, steeped in Whitman and ignited by him, fights back for his poetic life, partly by the Borgesian strategy (in advance of Borges) of *becoming* Walt Whitman, even as Borges' Pierre Menard became Cervantes in order to usurp the authorship of *Don Quixote*."[20] Or take his final sentence on the subject of an "Hispanic-Portuguese Whitman": "The ultimate lesson of Whitman's influence—on Borges, Neruda, Paz, and so many more— may be that only an originality as outrageous as Pessoa's could hope to contain it without hazard to the poetic self or selves."[21] Of course, Pessoa, like Whitman, contains "multitudes," and the Whitmanian aspect of Pessoa, important as it is, remains, after all, only one avenue into what is one of the most remarkable poetic canons in the history of Western poetry.

From the start Fernando Pessoa was a poet's poet— beginning, in Portugal, with his contemporaries and friends Mário de Sá-Carneiro, António Ferro, and Armando Côrtes-Rodrigues, moving through José Régio and Adolfo Casais Monteiro in the early 1930s, to, closer to our own day, Jorge de Sena and David Mourão-Ferreira. The English-language poets, whose culture he shared through schooling and to whose literary tradition he had hoped to belong, have been no exception in this. John Hollander, C.K. Williams, W.S. Merwin, and Mark Strand, along with the novelist and biographer Edmund White, have spoken of Pessoa's important place in modern poetry. White, while recognizing in Pessoa a "repressed homosexual" and a "discreet alcoholic," calls him "the most renowned Portuguese poet of this century," one who "divided himself into several different writers by some weird principle of poetic mitosis."[22] Hollander calls Pessoa "a great poet," concluding, in a 1987 review of Edwin Honig's and Susan M. Brown's Pessoa translations, that "anybody who cares about poetry, about fictions of identity, about the whole of modernism, must be grateful" for these translations.[23] At about the same time, Mark Strand, a former poet laureate, writes:

Fernando Pessoa is the least known of the masters of twentieth-century poetry. From his heteronymic passion he produced, if that is the word, two of our greatest poets, Alberto Caeiro and Álvaro de Campos, and a third, Ricardo Reis, who isn't bad. Pessoa is the exemplary poet of the self as other, of the poem as testament to unreality, proclamation of nothingness, occasion for expectancy.[24]

C.K. Williams calls Pessoa "one of the very great poets of the twentieth century" and "one of the fascinating figures of all literature, with his manifold identities, his amazing audacities, his brilliance and his shyness"; he concludes that "he is, in some ways, *the* poet of modernism, the only one willing to fracture himself into the parcels of action, anguish, and nostalgia which are the grounds of our actual situation."[25] W.S. Merwin, whose knowledge of Pessoa's work dates back at least to the 1950s, calls the Portuguese poet "one of the great originals (a fact rendered more striking by his writing as several distinct personalities) of the European poetry of the first part of this century."[26] And then there is Cyril Connolly, who produced a novel metaphor for Pessoa's heteronymy—he "hived off separate personalities like swarms of bees"—as he sought for Pessoa's "shade in those Edwardian cafés in Lisbon which he haunted, for he was Lisbon's Cavafy or Verlaine."[27]

In the long run, of course, Pessoa's reputation or lasting fame will depend on how future poets and scholars respond to his work. In the English-speaking world, that reputation has already been shaped and nurtured by the Pessoa-inspired poems of John Wain and Allen Ginsberg, Andrew Harvey and Michael Hamburger, Edwin Honig, and the Anglo-Israeli Dennis Silk. They have done their good work on Pessoa's behalf by encountering him (and sometimes emulating him) in poetry that is both critical and celebratory. If one result of their work is that the American critic can now put forth Pessoa's name as one of those whose work is likely to last from our "Chaotic Age,"[28] another might be the offhand, curiously Pessoan allusion one finds, not merely in the drawings of Benoit van Innis, but also elsewhere: in Joseph Brodsky's advice to readers of the *New York Times*, especially those with Portuguese, to read their Pessoa or in Armand Schwerner's "Old Dog Sermon:"

> for pain centuries
> our poems body the 'task,'
> Rilke calls it, chances between
> the harpoon and the hole—verbal gestures, paleoelectricity
> Blake
> Whitman, Fernando Pessoa, George Oppen—but among
> rare poem-epiphanies, gift
> dharma flutings, the uninhabitable
> otherness, werewolf Sahara
> of London Lisbon San Francisco the
> coffee house the campus auditorium[29]

Or consider what I take to be the veiled allusion to Pessoa and his coterie of four imagined poets in *Spell #7*, a play by Ntozake Shange, the acclaimed American poet with rediscovered roots in Africa: "when the japanese red army invaded san juan / they poisoned the papaya with portuguese. i eat a lotta papaya. last week / I developed a strange schizophrenic condition / with 4 manifest personalities: one spoke english & understood nothing / one spoke french & had access to the world / one spoke spanish & voted against statehood for puerto rico / one spoke portuguese, 'eu não falo ingles então y voce' / i dont speak english anymore / & you?"[30]

When Pessoa lay dying in the Hospital de São Luís dos Franceses in 1935 he set down what turned out to be his last words. In English he wrote, "I know not what tomorrow will bring"—he was echoing, consciously, I think, scripture that reads, "Boast not thyself of tomorrow; for thou knowest not what a day may bring forth" (Proverbs 27:1). That long "to-morrow" that concerned him did not bring him or his work the oblivion or "inexistence" that others, in his place, might have expected and feared. What the long future brought him was fame and ever-increasing acclaim, a just portion of which now comes, as it should, from the English-speaking world.

2

Old School Loyalties

Roy Campbell

"It was a Portuguese sailor who first put South Africa on the geographical map. It was a Portuguese who first put South Africa on the literary map. And it's a later Portuguese poet who was educated in Durban, who may claim to be the greatest literary figure of modern times."[1] So begins Roy Campbell, poet and translator, in a radio program over the South African Broadcasting Corporation in 1954. The sailor is Vasco de Gama, the poets, Luís de Camões and Fernando Pessoa. An ardent admirer of the Iberian countries and a staunch supporter of their fascist governments, Campbell had recently moved to Portugal to take up farming.

From the late 1920s to the late 1930s, Roy Campbell was commonly ranked with the best poets of his generation. His poetic strengths (and perhaps his greatest weakness) were evident from the start, as the American poet-critic Babette Deutsch, writing in 1931, discerned:

Irony gone savage and spiked with satire marks the work of Roy Campbell, the South African poet who will be remembered for the stormy incandescence of his first book, *The Flaming Terrapin*, which was, incidentally, a narrative poem. His second volume, *Adamastor*, exhibits the same fiery vigor, but the contents are brief and bitter lyrics. His verse is a kind of catapult, an elaborate magnificent engine, hurling its slings alike against Georgian poetasters and South African journalists, the lewd gross vulgus and the pink-eyed aesthete, the British empire-builders and the Dutch colonials. He is capable of exquisite lyrical flights—'The Palm' is one of them—and his imagery has splendor as well as violence, but he trains his guns in too many different directions, so that one is likely rather to admire his vehemence than to share his emotion.[2]

19

The historical importance of Campbell's work through the 1930s is still reflected in *Poetry of the 1930s* in 1967. Allan Rodway's anthology, which is limited to eight poets, puts Campbell in the company of W. H. Auden, Stephen Spender, C. Day Lewis, Louis Macneice, Dylan Thomas, George Barker, and David Gascoyne despite its editor's obvious disapproval of Campbell's politics. "Apart from Ezra Pound (living in Italy)," he writes, "he was the only poet of any merit to express fascist sympathies— and indeed to fight for Franco in the Spanish Civil War."[3] But Rodway's fairness to Campbell, however reluctant, is atypical. Most of Campbell's readers were less ready to put aside his unpopular, vociferously held conservative (if not reactionary) politics when judging his poetry, with the result that by 1957, when he died, Campbell's literary reputation had declined severely. The powerful literary establishment of the Left had done its work early, always holding Campbell (as it seldom did T.S. Eliot, William Butler Yeats, and even Ezra Pound) closely accountable for his politics, offering caricature and general accusation rather than analysis or aesthetic evaluation. In *Mithraic Emblems* (1936), for example, an anonymous reviewer in *New Verse* sees "Mr. Bullfighter Campbell in a ridiculous parody of himself in many swaggering, snorting, boring poems. A dotty idealism. Big swelling muscles holding up highly coloured bladders of bad air."[4] Three years later another anonymous review in *New Verse* builds on this view. It dismisses *Flowering Rifle* as a "monster of a poem":

Flowering Rifle is rough, noisy, and, line by line, adroit. It is very long and very clumsily arranged. It emphasizes and repeats and repeats . . . . [I]t is written in literature-language, containing no illustration or image from anything honestly and individually and newly experienced. Energetic, it simply glorifies energetic Fascism in Spain, with plenty of energetic Jew-baiting, and energetic boasting. Energy fascinates one to a certain morbid degree, but it is a quality exercised, without moral checks, by weasels, dung-beetles and dictators. It is no more admirable, by itself or when badly directed, than sincerity.[5]

The end result of attacks such as these is evident in Robin Skelton's *Poetry of the Thirties* (1964), an inclusive anthology issued by Penguin. Forty-six British poets are represented, but

Campbell is missing. Not only is his work not represented, but he goes unmentioned in the twenty-five-page historical introduction. The current edition of the *Norton Anthology of Modern Poetry* omits Campbell. As one of his more sympathetic critics explains, "[Campbell's] particular poetic virtues do not place him in any kind of group or movement for which there is a current vogue, and it is more than likely that he will remain, for the moment at least, a poetic outsider, just as he lived most of his life as a human outsider."[6] In this context it is worth quoting the assessment of Campbell by the Southern African novelist and critic Alan Paton. He notes:

It is the modern custom to denigrate Campbell and his poetry. He wrote some very foolish poetry, and some equally foolish prose. Many readers of this foolish poetry and prose were so incensed that they failed to recognize two things—one was that Campbell wrote half-a-dozen of the finest lyrics of the twentieth century, and the other was that no twentieth century poet could rival Campbell's vigor, his mastery of imagery, and his use of sound and color.[7]

Also contributing to the devaluation and neglect of Campbell as a British poet is that after the disappointing reviews of *Talking Bronco* (1946) he turned his hand largely to nonfictional prose and translation. In fact, what is left of his literary reputation now rests largely on his translations from the French, Spanish, and Portuguese.

Campbell felt that he was an inspired translator. Of his *Poems of Saint John of the Cross*, for example, he boasted that "the Saint only needed to raise his stick and say '*Arré burro!*' ['Gee up, donkey!'] to me, and the Donkey trotted."[8] He made distinguished translations of Charles Baudelaire's *Les fleurs du mal* and of Federico García Lorca's *Romancero gitano*. From the Portuguese Campbell translated the early poets Gil Vicente and Luís Vaz de Camões, the nineteenth-century poets Bocage and Antero de Quental, and the twentieth-century poets José Régio, Carlos Queiroz, Joaquim Paço d'Arcos, and Fernando Pessoa. Much of this work he intended for an anthology of Portuguese poetry, which did not materialize but was incorporated in essays and in *Portugal*, a book published in the year of his death. He also turned his hand to the translation, more or less

successfully, of the nineteenth-century novels of Eça de Quei-
rós: he published *Cousin Bazilio* (*O primo Basílio*) in 1953 and
The City and the Mountains (*A cidade e as serras*) in 1955.[9]

Born in South Africa in 1901, Campbell, like Fernando
Pessoa, was educated in Durban schools. They attended the
same school, in fact, though not at the same time, since Pessoa
was a dozen years older than Campbell. Years later, when
Campbell discovered the work of the great Portuguese modernist and learned the details of his life, he remembered having seen Pessoa's name carved on a desk at the Durban High
School. Campbell "did not see the name [of Pessoa] again till
years after; but," he recalled, "I sat before it for six months and
recognised it at once: since whenever I was in a brown study I
used to focus on the name, 'F. Pessoa.'"[10]

It was not Pessoa, however, who first brought Campbell to
Portuguese literature. In 1926 he discovered *Os Lusíadas* in
William Julius Mickle's 1776 translation and recognized it as
one of the great epic poems in Western literature.[11] He praised
one of Edith Sitwell's books by telling her: "I keep [it] beside my
bed along with San Juan de la Cruz and Luís de Camões. It is
about the only book of English verse published for a century
that can hold its own in such company."[12] In 1930 he had entitled his fourth book of poems *Adamastor,* a reference, he explained, to "the spirit of the Cape whose apparition and pro-
phecy form one of the finest passages in 'The Lusiad[s]' of
Camoëns."[13] This volume includes "Rounding the Cape," another celebration of Camões's creation. Later Campbell also
extols Camões's courageous spirit and tough bravery and identifies with him, regarding him as "a comrade where I sought a
master," one who could "look a common soldier in the face."[14]
For him, as he later explained, "[Camões] is the soldier's poet
par excellence."[15]

But Campbell reserved his greatest admiration for Camões's
poetry of the sea around southern Africa. Calling him "the
greatest of all South African poets," Campbell insists that only
Camões "gives one in words a real sense of its awe and the
grandeur of its stormy seas [of 'going round Agulhas (or the
Needles) to the Cape itself'] . . . in that wonderful passage about
Rounding the Cape."[16] There is nothing surprising, of course, in
Campbell's assessment of Camões as a poet of the sea. More sur-

prising is Pessoa's appeal to Campbell as a South African sea poet; Campbell found in him "a modern throw-back to Camões, and one of the greatest marine poets of all times, along with Homer, Melville, Corbière, and Camões."[17] And that "very ocean, as Fernando Pessoa, greatest of modern poets, writes in *Mensagem*," notes Campbell, "is salt with the tears of Portuguese widows, mothers and sweethearts, who have lost their husbands, sons or lovers at sea or overseas."[18] It is something of a tribute to Campbell that the 1989 edition of the *Penguin Book of Southern African Verse* opens with Camões's *Os Lusíadas*, Canto V, in Sir Richard Fanshawe's translation, and includes five poems by Fernando Pessoa.

In 1937, on his way to the war in Spain, Campbell and his wife made an extended visit to Portugal, where they took up temporary residence in Sesimbra. One of their visits while in Portugal was to Sintra, the famous resort town to the north of Lisbon. Later, in 1952 when he decided to settle in Portugal, Campbell remembered that pleasant visit and eventually rented a small farm called "Gurgling Farm" (Quinta dos Bochechos) in Galamares, near Sintra. In that first year in Portugal, besides finishing up his translation of Baudelaire and a critical book on García Lorca, he worked at translating Eça's *O primo Basílio*. Campbell's biographer calls his efforts at this time "still very imperfect," for "he had to use a dictionary constantly."[19] In 1954, besides translating plays by Lope de Vega, Calderón de la Barca, Lorca, and Tirso de Molina for the BBC, he worked away at his translation of Eça's *A cidade e as serras*, doing as much as forty pages a day. He had also agreed, as he had mentioned in his radio broadcast, to write a small book on Fernando Pessoa for the Cambridge publisher Bowes and Bowes. But in early 1955 circumstances compelled Campbell to change his plans. The Campbells decided to give up Bochechos. They had neglected to insure their workers, and when one of them was injured seriously, they were obliged to pay not only his hospital bills but also "an amount equal to two-thirds of his monthly wage for the rest of his life."[20] At this time Campbell revived an old project. He secured a grant from the Portuguese government to tour Portugal in preparation for writing a book on the country. He finished the book, entitled *Portugal*, in early 1957, and Pessoa holds a prominent place in it. After surveying more than five centuries of Portuguese poetry, Campbell reaches Pessoa, whom he introduces: "We shall have to give that amazing poet Fernando Pessoa a space to himself."[21] He gives Pessoa substantial space—four pages—two and a half of which present Pessoa's poetry in Campbell's translation. Appearing in early 1957, these pages constitute one of the early efforts to introduce Pessoa's work to an English-language audience.[22] Not until 1952, in fact, had Pessoa been introduced into the *Oxford Book of Portuguese Verse*.[23] Two-thirds of B. Vidigal's editorial note is devoted to Pessoa. It concludes emphatically that "the acceptance of Pessoa was a step forward in dispelling the prejudice against the so-called modernist poetry."[24]

Within months of completing his book on *Portugal,* Roy Campbell was killed in an accident in Setubal. He left unfulfilled his agreement with Bowes and Bowes of London for a book on Pessoa. In 1960, João Gaspar Simões, Pessoa's first biographer, agreed to write such a book at the request of Campbell's widow.[25] Simões tells the story in various places, but nowhere does he mention that Campbell had made a substantial beginning on his biocritical introduction to Pessoa. Perhaps Simões was unaware of it.

But Campbell's 1954 radio broadcast gives us a sense of what he intended to write in his book on Pessoa. His approach would be direct, clear, sure-handed. Pessoa, he said, was

scarcely noticed by those with whom he came in contact, so shy was he, and so insignificant he seemed externally. Yet this single author, a great poet while writing under his own name, projected five other poets under different heteronyms—each with a style as distinctive and personal as his own. He gave them such reality that he even wrote letters and replies from one another of these fictitious poets as if they really existed in the flesh, with temperaments and styles as different from his own as his was from his contemporaries, and all as great as he was himself in the poems that he wrote under his own name. The fact is that his external shyness and insignificance was offset by an internal creative intensity for which a single style and personality were insufficient, and so he projected these several other poets out of his personality—just as Shakespeare projected the Lears, the Caesars, the Antonies and Hamlets of his plays, all equal to himself in the soarings of their intellect or in the forces of their emotions.[26]

In typical fashion Campbell seized the moment to advertise his next two books, which he had probably already begun, for at his death he left in a notebook drafts of two entire chapters and the substantial portion of a third chapter of his book on Pessoa. Campbell's text breaks off with a translation of some hundred lines from Álvaro de Campos's "Ode marítima." This excerpt from the poem Campbell described as "the loudest poem ever written" more than doubles the number of lines from the poem Campbell published in his lifetime.[27] These also appear to constitute an earlier version of Campbell's efforts to translate Pessoa's poem than the forty-five lines he published in *Portugal* (1957). Elsewhere in Campbell's workbooks there are attempts at translating Álvaro de Campos's "Ah, um Soneto" and "Opiário" (bits of stanzas 1 and 2), along with, from the orthonymic *Mensagem*, three versions of "Mar português" and two versions of "O Mostrengo" (both differing from the excerpt that appears in his Pessoa manuscript). There is also a sentence that seems to refer to Pessoa and his heteronyms. Written on a single sheet torn from a notebook, it reads: "The very opposite of Valery who declared that it was impossible for him to write on a blank sheet 'The Marchioness went out at five o'clock,' this poet here began by creating multitudes of fictional figures by means of which he hoped to disguise his own features."[28]

Campbell started his Pessoa manuscript in the 1950s, though it cannot be dated more precisely. His rather hostile references to the character of the English adventurer-writer T.E. Lawrence, accompanied by contrasts drawn between Lawrence's and Pessoa's sexual proclivities—a good bit of it fanciful and digressive in a book on Pessoa—suggest that the writing of chapter 2 took place in 1954, much of it during mid-summer.

Campbell's long-standing hatred of Lawrence, well entrenched by the 1950s, deserves some comment. Among Campbell's papers there is a note, probably from 1954, that provides some background for his pronouncements on Lawrence:

When it comes out I would like to review that book of [Richard] Aldington about the greatest fraud in English history: T.E. Lawrence. I may seem ungrateful. He got my first book published. I have got his mail. He was going to hoist me into fame. When I told him that I was a

man, that I was married at the age of 19—he hated me: he wrote fren-
zied insults and fell in love with my wife's Lesbian Sister who is about
6 feet high.[29]

When Aldington's book, critical of Lawrence, came under heavy
attack, Campbell's anger flared up. He wanted to speak up in defense of his friend Aldington, but this "project, like so many
others Campbell engaged in, came to nothing," writes his biographer, "because of the danger of a libel suit."[30] His frustration
at not being able to defend Aldington, coming when he was
trying to write his book on Pessoa, might help to explain why
T.E. Lawrence gets bootlegged into a book about a Portuguese
poet who had no connection with him or his work.[31]

In judging the quality of Campbell's unfinished and un-
revised manuscript, one must recognize that the author's intention was modest. He wanted merely to introduce, to an
English-language audience, "one of the strangest personalities
in the history of literature," a poet writing in a language not
considered to be among the major languages of Europe.[32] To
make his observations meaningful, Campbell seizes every opportunity to compare Pessoa's work with that of English,
American, and other Continental European writers of acknowledged and unquestioned stature. Because Pessoa was a new
name to English-language readers, Campbell felt encouraged to
lean heavily on Portuguese scholarship, especially the pioneering work of João Gaspar Simões, published in 1950, and the in-
cisive criticism of Adolfo Casais Monteiro throughout the 1930s
and 1940s. To recognize this dual dependence on Gaspar Simões and Casais Monteiro, however, is not to suggest that Campbell's book—what we have of it—is unoriginal. On the contrary,
Campbell's view of Pessoa, in what he chooses to emphasize,
both in the life and in the work he values most, is distinctly his.
Using tone and calculated interpolation to augment and orches-
trate argument, Campbell leaves his own unmistakable imprint
on the work. To illustrate the point, one need only consider
Campbell's historical defense of the Portuguese soldier's accom-
plishments and valor, his interpolated personal anecdote on the
shenanigans of the diabolist Aleister Crowley, or his extended
discussion of T.E. Lawrence as sadist and charlatan. Unfortun-

ately, Campbell does not go beyond accounting for the heteronym Álvaro de Campos. What he would have done with Ricardo Reis, Alberto Caeiro, or the orthonymic English-language poetry is not apparent from the chapters he has left us. We do know from another source, however, that he disliked Pessoa's English-language work.[33]

Campbell's manuscript on Pessoa, like his *Portugal*, is very much a work of the early 1950s. It is staunchly pro-Salazar. Campbell's view of *Mensagem* as a *saudosista* poem, one powerfully consonant with the views and aims of the *Estado Novo*, must have gratified Pessoa's old friend of the days of *Orpheu* António Ferro, the Director of SNI (the ministry for information and propaganda). It was Ferro who had made certain that Pessoa's poetic sequence shared the first Antero de Quental Prize for Poetry in 1934. After all, politics notwithstanding, *Mensagem* was the work, as Campbell insisted, of "the finest poet in any language of this half-century."[34]

3

Poet and Antipoet

Edouard Roditi and Thomas Merton

Credit Edouard Roditi with having introduced Fernando Pessoa to readers in the United States. Poet, scholar, and translator, Roditi was an American born in Paris in 1910. In a "conversation with Edmund White," published in 1985, he recalled:

My father was an American citizen, though born as a Sephardic Jew in Constantinople and then educated here in Paris before ever going to the United States. Later, as an American citizen, he ran a buying office here in Paris for American department stores and was a member of the American Chamber of Commerce. My mother was English and I was born in Paris, grew up here as a child and was sent at the age of nine to boarding schools in England, so that I visited the United States for the first time only briefly, when I was nineteen, then again as briefly in 1932. I lived in America continuously only from 1937 until 1946, but I now return there every year for several months.[1]

Roditi was educated at Balliol College, Oxford, in 1927-1928 and at the University of Chicago, where he received his B.A. in 1939. During World War II he was affiliated with the Voice of America in New York, and after the war he served as an interpreter at the war crimes trials in Nuremberg. On occasion he taught literature, briefly, at such places as San Francisco State University and Brown University. He was the author of several volumes of poetry; books on Oscar Wilde, Joachim Karsch, Magellan, and Joseph Conrad; and several collections of tales and essays.[2] He was also a translator. In the words of Thomas Epstein, "A polyglot, Roditi wrote fluently in at least four modern languages and translated poetry from more than a dozen languages *into* three different languages; as for prose, he wrote that he 'translated from so many different languages that I should modestly blush, were I called upon to list in greater detail the full range of these five-finger exercises.'"[3] The writers Roditi translated include André Breton, Albert Memmi, Ernest Namenyi, Yashar Kemal, Pablo Picasso, and Robert Schmutzler. In an autobiographical account written shortly before his death in 1992, he complained that while the French sometimes included him in their collections of American poetry, American critics invariably excluded him, setting him aside as a European writer.

Roditi's knowledge of Portuguese led to his work with the poet Paul Celan in the 1950s on translations into German of Fernando Pessoa's poems. Seven such translations appeared in *Die Neue Rundschau* in 1956, introduced with an essay by Roditi.[4] Roditi's introduction draws on work done earlier in Portuguese and lays the basis for later essays in Portuguese and English. "The Several Names of Fernando Pessoa," a succinct five-page article that appeared in *Poetry* magazine in October 1955, is the first piece of criticism on Pessoa published in the United States. It was followed, eight years later, by the publication in the *Literary Review* of "Fernando Pessoa, Outsider Among English Poets," which also presents a sampling of Pessoa's English-language poetry: ten of the *35 Sonnets*, *Epithalamium* (parts 1 and 2), and three epitaphs from "Inscriptions."[5] Pessoa was well served in the 1950s by Roditi's thoughtful, knowledgeable, and penetrating work on his behalf. Roditi's essays touch on most of the important critical and biographical matters.

Given Roditi's early acquaintance with Pessoa's writing and his initiative in presenting it to the readership of *Poetry* magazine, it seems remarkable that Roditi clearly shows signs of having been influenced by Pessoa only in work published posthumously. Two Pessoan poems by Roditi appear in *World Letter* in 1993. Dedicated to Roditi, this fourth issue of the magazine features Roditi as poet and translator. Besides translations from the French of Alain Bosquet and from the Portuguese of Miguel Torga, there are examples of Roditi's own poetry. The title of one poem recalls unequivocally "Autopsicografia," Pessoa's quintessential statement-poem published toward the end of his life:

Autopsychoanalysis
What Minotaur lurks in the heart
Of the labyrinth I nightly tread,
And who can ever unravel the meaning
Of the Maginogion of my dreams.

Each morning, pasty-mouthed, I awake
From memories of past frustrations
So compounded that I soon forget
All but their setting, a long-lost home

That haunts me, but strangely transformed,
As if none other that ever housed me
On either shore of an ocean had left
A more lasting imprint in my memory.

Homeless now from having lived in too many
Homes, I'm everywhere a stranger
Save in a distant past, a lost
Childhood and boyhood paradise.[6]

Pessoa's "Autopsicografia," first published in the journal *Presença* in November 1932, reads:

The poet is that forger who
Forges so completely that
He forges even the feeling
He feels truly as pain.

And those who read his poems
Feel absolutely, not his two
Separate pains, but only the
Pain that they do not feel.

And thus, diverting the
Understanding, the wind-up
Train we call the heart
Runs along its track.[7]

Like Pessoa's, Roditi's poem is less an analysis of the work-
ings of the psyche or of the self than an explanation or apologia
for a life (or its description) that, as it turned out, was nearly

over. While Pessoa focuses on the complexity of feeling and art that arises out of feeling and that creates emotion to create emotion, along with the relative meaninglessness of the whole project, given the nature of human existence, Roditi looks back over a life lived that has been nomadic, perhaps psychologically splintering. In this, Roditi moves a good deal away from the Portuguese poet who lived his entire adult life in Lisbon and her immediate environs and toward Jorge de Sena, another Portuguese poet who was more nomadic than Pessoa (but less so than Roditi). It is Sena's centrally modern poem, "In Crete, with the Minotaur," that Roditi draws on, perhaps without full consciousness, for his metaphor of the labyrinth and the human beast therein and for the notion that he is "Homeless now from having lived in too many / Homes," "everywhere a stranger / Save," that is, "in a distant past, a lost / childhood and boyhood paradise." Here Roditi echoes the Pessoa who dreams of his lost childhood in "Oblique Rain" ("Chuva oblíqua") or "Tripe— Porto Style" ("Dobrada à moda do Porto").

In Roditi's other poem in World Letter, "The Warning," we find echoes of Pessoa's English-language poems, particularly his sonnets, both in the sentiment expressed in the last quatrain and in the coinage of "no-being" (with apologies to T.S. Eliot's "Love Song of J. Alfred Prufrock" —"I am no prophet—and here's no great matter; / I have seen the moment of my greatness flicker, / And I have seen the eternal Footman hold my coat, and snicker / And in short, I was afraid").

> I've wandered in nebulous regions of limbo
> From which one returns, if at all,
> Only forewarned, with a knowledge of death
> Briefly vouchsafed in a feverish trance.
>
> Forever this foretaste of death must now haunt,
> Whether awake or in dreams, my scarred mind
> While my ill that's the Idiot's repeatedly apes
> My first painful acquaintance with space and with time.
>
> Though no prophet, I've often felt warned that my end
> Must close like a bracket this pause that began
> With my birth's other bracket in the ceaseless flow
> Of no-being that's bound by no space and no time.[8]

Here one might quote lines from the last of Pessoa's *35 Sonnets:* "The outer day, void statue of lit blue, / Is altogether outward, other, glad / At mere being not-I."[9]

But the Pessoa poem that stands most firmly behind Roditi's two poems is another poem from his *35 Sonnets,* ten of which Roditi reproduced in the *Literary Review* in 1963.[10] Pessoa numbers it sonnet 18. It is not included by Roditi, though he does include the sonnets that immediately precede and follow it, that is to say, sonnets 17 and 19.

> Indefinite space, which, by co-substance night,
> In one black mystery two void mysteries blends;
> The stray stars, whose innumerable light
> Repeats one mystery till conjecture ends;
> The stream of time, known by birth-bursting bubbles;
> The gulf of silence, empty even of nought;
> Thought's high-walled maze, which the outed owner troubles
> Because the string's lost and the plan forgot:
> When I think on this and that here I stand,
> The thinker of these thoughts, emptily wise,
> Holding up to my thinking my thing-hand
> And looking at it with thought-alien eyes,
>   My wonder at my wonder looketh past
>   The universal darkness lone and vast.[11]

Discussing Pessoa's penchant in his English poems for expressing "his metaphysical considerations and erotic fantasies in somewhat learned diction, creating for himself an idiom as personal as," to speak of only two English poets, that of William Blake or Gerard Manley Hopkins, Roditi called the English poet Pessoa "one of the hermits of our language, a kind of Trappist of English poetry."[12] I would not argue that the matter was in any way directly connected with Roditi's characterization of Pessoa, but in 1966, the American poet and Trappist monk Thomas Merton published a batch of translations from the poetry of Fernando Pessoa—more specifically, a dozen poems by the heteronymic Alberto Caeiro. These translations were done originally to demonstrate to Daisetz Z. Suzuki that decades earlier there had existed a European poet in the guise of Pessoa's heteronym who had written poetry of "great Zen quality."[13] In

Pessoa, Merton had also found a poet who, like San Juan de la Cruz, was capable of describing "the dark night."[14] Earlier, in a dialogue with Suzuki published in 1961, Merton had glossed the efficient uses of the Spanish mystic's "doctrine of 'night'":

If we are to die to ourselves and live "in Christ," does that not mean that we must somehow find ourselves "dead" and "empty" with regard to our old self? If we are to be moved in all things by the grace of Christ should we not in some sense realize this as action out-of-emptiness, springing from the mystery of the pure freedom which is "divine love," rather than as something produced in and with our egotistical, exterior self, springing from our desires and referred to our own spiritual interest?[15]

It is this matter of emptying out and subsequent "action out-of-emptiness" that links Saint John of the Cross with Zen, for "the man who has truly found his spiritual nakedness, who has realized he is empty, is not a self that has *acquired* emptiness or *become* empty. He just 'is empty from the beginning,' as Dr. Suzuki has observed. . . . He is one with God and identified with God and hence knows nothing of any ego in himself. All he knows is love."[16] In Zen, Merton explained to Suzuki, he found "the very atmosphere of the Gospels, and the Gospels are bursting with it."[17] To prove his point, Merton translated some of Alberto Caeiro's poems, working from some of Octavio Paz's Spanish translations as well as the originals. "I spoke to Dr. Suzuki, the Zen master [during their visit at Columbia University], about Pessoa and translated some poems of his for S. (from the Spanish of Octavio Paz)," he wrote in 1964, "and S. was delighted. Said it had a great Zen quality. I think so too."[18] On June 30, 1964, Merton wrote to the Nicaraguan poet and journalist Pablo Antonio Cuadra: "Ernesto [Cardenal] sent me Octavio Paz's translations of Fernando Pessoa and I am very much taken with his poetry. I am looking for the originals and expect to do some translating of that. Pessoa is very congenial to me in his existentialism. Very Zen-like also."[19] Obviously Merton had not yet settled on the versions of Pessoa's poems he had done for Suzuki, for on September 26, he wrote to the Nicaraguan poet Ernesto Cardenal: "Have been reading Pessoa, in *Spanish and Portuguese* (thanks for sending the Paz translations) and he is a real discovery. I like him very much and may attempt some translations for New Directions. I think I told you I had read some Pessoa to Suzuki and he was delighted with it."[20] In his journal, on June 20, 1964, he had written with satisfaction:

I sat with Suzuki on the sofa and we talked of all kinds of things to do with Zen and with life. He read to me from a Chinese text, the Blue Cliff collection, I think, familiar stories on Zen. I translated to him selections from Octavio Paz's Spanish version of Fernando Pessoa. There were a few things in Pessoa he liked immensely (especially "Praise be to God that I am not good"—"That is so important," said Suzuki with great feeling).[21]

When, in 1965, Merton gave Caeiro's poems to Hiromu Morishita, a survivor of the Hiroshima bombing, he wrote him a note thanking him for some calligraphies and poems: "I am very grateful to you. I am enclosing some poems which I recently translated from Portuguese [of Fernando Pessoa]. They lack the delicacy and suggestiveness of Japanese poetry, but contain something of the Japanese view of things, I believe. I have been reading the philosopher Nishida Kitaro, a great man, and these poems have something of his outlook."[22] In the same year Merton published his translations of a dozen poems from Alberto Caeiro's *O guardador de rebanhos,* calling it *The Keeper of the Flocks.* This little book was published by the Abbey of Our Lady of Gethsemani in Trappist, Kentucky. In 1966 Merton's translations of Caeiro received wider dissemination when they appeared in *ND: New Directions in Prose and Poetry 19,* with the following translator's note:

Fernando Pessoa (1888-1935) is a curious and original figure of the early twentieth century, in some sense an antipoet, who wrote under several pseudonymns in Portuguese besides publishing poems in English and Portuguese over his own name. These twelve poems are from a collection, *The Keeper of the Flocks,* attributed by Pessoa to a fictitious personage called Alberto Caeiro—and the first line of the book is "I am not a keeper of the flocks." The interest of the poetic (or anti-poetic) experience of Alberto Caeiro lies in its Zen-like immediacy, though this is sometimes complicated by a certain note of self-conscious and programmatic insistence. However, Pessoa-Caeiro may

be numbered among those Western writers who have expressed something akin to the Zen way of seeing—the "knack of full awareness."[23]

Merton's description of Pessoa as an antipoet encourages us to
link him closely to Merton the poet in the mid to late 1960s. As
he wrote to Hiromu Morishita in 1967, just after his book
Cables to the Ace appeared, "It is perhaps a time of 'anti-poems,'
and I have lately translated some such 'anti-poems' by a friend
of mine in Chile, Nicanor Parra." His own antipoetic book
Merton described as "largely experimental . . . [it] may be hard
to understand, full of ironies and ambiguities appropriate to the
moment when we are saturated with the wrong kind of communication."[24] Merton aspired to the antipoetry of Nicanor Parra.
He called him the poet of "the dry, disconcerting voice . . . the
poet of the sneeze,"[25] an observation reminiscent of Álvaro
de Campos's complaint, "I have a terrible cold. / And everyone
knows how terrible colds / Change the whole structure of the
universe, / Making us sore at life, / Making us sneeze till we get
metaphysical."[26] And Merton aspired to the poetry of the heteronymic Alberto Caeiro. He sounds like the Caeiro of the first
and final stages—though not of the middle stage—when he
quotes toward the end of his "Postface" to *Zen and the Birds of
Appetite* the "Zen saying: before I grasped Zen, the mountains
were nothing but mountains and the rivers nothing but rivers.
When I got into Zen, the mountains were no longer mountains
and the rivers no longer rivers. But when I understood Zen, the
mountains were only mountains and the rivers only rivers."[27]
Here is a Zen-like Caeiro, in Merton's translation:

> Whenever I look at things and think
> What men think about them,
> I laugh like the stream
> Falling with a cool sound
> Over the stones.
> For the only hidden meaning things have
> Is that they have no hidden meaning.
> Stranger than all that is strange,
> Than poets' dreams and philosophical ideas
> Is this: things are actually
> Just what they appear to be
> And there is nothing about them to understand.

> Yes, here is what my senses learned
> All by themselves:
> Things do not have meanings: they have existence.
> Things are the only hidden meanings of things.[28]

Or as Caeiro says in another poem translated by Merton, "in the end, the stars are stars only / And flowers are flowers only / Which is why we call them / Stars and flowers."[29] Parra, as Merton saw, was "sharp, hard, full of solid irony," a "no-nonsense anti-poet with a deep sense of the futility and corruption of social life."[30] So strong were the similarities Merton saw in Pessoa and Parra as antipoets that he even contemplated putting them together in a single book. He confided to his journal on January 27, 1965: "Maybe I will do a book of translations from Parra and Pessoa and call it 'Two Anti-Poets.' I think I will write [James] Laughlin [of New Directions] about this."[31]

Merton's linking of Alberto Caeiro with San Juan de la Cruz, however, counters the usual view of the temperament of Pessoa's heteronym. For according to Campos, who was his disciple, Caeiro was not a pagan poet but paganism itself. Indeed Merton's linking of the two poets replies before the fact to the views put forth by two other students of Caeiro's poetry. In 1968 Jorge de Sena, ever suspicious of religions in which claims are made for direct communication with the "divine," also linked up the Spanish mystic with Caeiro, writing: "I always found that the mystics, as Alberto Caeiro would say, were sick poets, or worse, poets who did not know that they were such—and the case of San Juan de la Cruz is, in this regard, the most typical of the monumentally stupid from the vantage point of intelligence."[32] A year later, the English poet-critic Michael Hamburger, in *The Truth of Poetry*, concluded: "Caeiro's pantheism is one that can finally dispense with God, giving back God's attributes and glory to the visible world."[33] To illustrate his point, Hamburger quotes Caeiro:

But if God is trees and flowers
And mountains and moonlight and sun
Why do I call him God?
I call him flowers and trees and mountains and sun and moonlight;

For if, so that I can see him,
He turns himself into sun and moonlight and flowers and
    mountains and trees,
If he appears to me as mountains and trees
And moonlight and sun and flowers,
It was his will that I should know him
As trees and mountains and flowers and moonlight and sun.[34]

Yet perhaps this discordance between San Juan de la Cruz and
Caeiro is more apparent than real, for as Merton would have
understood them, they fall within the boundaries set out by the
Spanish mystic poet:

> In order to have pleasure in everything
> Desire to have pleasure in nothing.
>
> In order to arrive at possessing everything
> Desire to possess nothing.
>
> In order to arrive at being everything
> Desire to be nothing.

And especially the last one:

> In order to arrive at knowing everything
> Desire to know nothing.[35]

In *The Ascent to Truth* (1951) Merton comments on these lines
in a way that might well accommodate the ascetic and, perhaps,
dark ways of Caeiro.

Todo y Nada. All or nothing. The two words contain the theology of
St. John of the Cross. Todo—all—is God, Who contains in Himself em-
inently the perfections of all things. For Him we are made. In Him we
possess all things. But in order to possess Him Who is all, we must re-
nounce the possession of anything that is less than God. But everything that can be seen, known, enjoyed, possessed in a finite manner, is
less than God. Every desire for knowledge, possession, being that falls
short of God must be blacked out. *Nada!*[36]

For Pessoa's critics the notion that Caeiro can be read within the tradition of sixteenth-century Christian mysticism might seem far-fetched, but it appears to have made perfectly good sense to Merton.

Yet it was not only Caeiro among Pessoa's heteronyms who attracted Merton. Although he neither translated nor at any time referred to the poems of Álvaro de Campos, which he could have read in Octavio Paz's translations (not to say in the original), it was that modernist, futurist poet who crops up as the gray eminence of Merton's 1968 volume of poetry and prose *Cables to the Ace.* Paz had started out his selection of Campos's poems with a version of his Whitmanian "Ode triunfal," but by 1968 Merton was presumably familiar with Campos's other Whitmanian poems as well, "Saudação a Walt Whitman" ("Salutation to Walt Whitman"), for example, especially lines such as these:

Walt, dearest old man, my great Comrade, *evohë!*
I belong to your bacchic orgy of freed sensations,
I am yours, from the tingling of my toes to the nausea of my dreams.
I am yours, look at me—up there close to God, you see me
    contrariwise,
From inside out . . . You divine my body, you see my soul—
You see it properly, and through its eyes you take in my body—
Look at me: you know that I, Álvaro de Campos, ship's engineer,
Sensationist poet,
Am not your disciple, am not your friend, am not your singer,
You know that I am You, and you are happy about it![37]

Caeiro-Campos-Whitman weighs in, with Ginsberg, Hart Crane, and Bob Dylan (the last a Merton favorite at the time), to enable Merton's cantankerous, ironic, even angry antipoetic *Cables to the Ace* (subtitled "Familiar Liturgies of Misunder-standing"), a work of mixed discourse and varied literary forms, which opens with this "Prologue" (dated May 1967):

> You, Reader, need no prologue. Do you think these
> Horatian Odes are all about you? Far from the new
> wine to need a bundle. You are no bundle. Go advertise
> yourself.

Why not more pictures? Why not more rhythms, melody, etc.? All suitable questions to be answered some other time. The realm of spirit is two doors down the hall. There you can obtain more soul than you are ready to cope with, Buster.
The poet has not announced these mosaics on purpose.
Furthermore he has changed his address and his poetics are on vacation.
He is not roaring in the old tunnel.
Go shake hands with the comics if you demand a preface.
My attitudes are common and my ironies are no less usual than the bright pages of your favorite magazine.
The soaps, the smells, the liquors, the insurance, the third, dull, gin-soaked cheer: what more do you want, Rabble?
Go write your own prologue.
I am the incarnation of everybody and the zones of
    reassurance.
I am the obstetrician of good fortune. I live in the social
    cages of joy.
It is morning, afternoon or evening. Begin.
I too have slept here in my stolen Cadillac.
I too have understudied the Paradise swan.[38]

With a familiar nod to the obstetrician (possibly William Carlos Williams), Merton echoes the Whitmanian Campos of "Triumphal Ode" ("Ah to be everybody and everywhere!") while insisting that he is "the incarnation of everybody." And just as he has brought Williams, it seems, into his poem, Merton later seems also to allude to Campos, the naval engineer trained in Glasgow:

> "Look! The Engineer! He thinks he has caught something! He wrestles with it in mid-air!"[39]

It was the antipoetic "Zen" poetry of Alberto Caeiro that had first attracted Merton, but *Cables to the Ace* suggests that he was touched as well by the Whitmanian noise of Álvaro de Campos. And why not? Was not there something of Merton's Caeiro in Campos, too? Take the Campos who wrote:

> Sometimes I have ideas, good ones,
> Ideas that are surprisingly good
> And which come to me in the notions
>   and words of their natural expression.
>
> I write them down, then I read them over.
> Why have I written this?
> Where did I dig this up?
> Where did it come from? This is better than I . . .
> Can it be that we worldlings are no more than the pen
>   and ink someone else employs
> To set down in full what we can only draft.[40]

Surely this Campos was not alien to the Merton who in *The Ascent to Truth* had written:

> The Master Himself does not waste time tuning the
> instruments. He shows His servant, reason, how to do it and
> leaves him to do the work. If He then comes and finds the
> piano still out of tune, He does not bother to play anything
> on it.[41]

Cables to the Ace was published in March 1968. Merton died in December of the same year in Bangkok.

4

Dominoes

Edwin Honig

Edwin Honig's first collection of translations from Pessoa had just appeared when he was asked, at a translators' convention, "When you devote a lot of time to a big project of somebody else's, do you find that some of that creeps into some of your own work?" His answer was direct:

Yes, I've translated two poets in my experience as a translator; at great length, that is, over great periods of time, Lorca and Pessoa. But I found that not only was one involved as one would be in the physical business of translating, but one would think, one would spend one's days thinking unconsciously in their language. . . .

There's little question of the temperamental affinity that you find, and it starts you off. . . . You use that language where everybody's singing his own tune and suddenly you hear someone singing your tune. You didn't know he existed, and you begin to sing along and then it becomes yours, it becomes more yours.[1]

Honig had first heard Pessoa's poems recited in an English bar in Praia da Rocha, first by a fisherman intoning "Mar português" and then by another customer who turned out to be the author of an early biocritical study of Pessoa. But "It was not until two summers later, in the dank cool of my basement billiard room in Cranston, Rhode Island," recalled Honig, twenty-five years later, "that a flywheel began to turn inside me, keeping time with the narrator's voice in *Ode Marítima*. It was there and in *Saudação a Walt Whitman* that I recognized the presence of Whitman's language-thrust and wideranging spirit."[2] The Pessoan voice that first attracted Honig was that of Álvaro de Campos at its raucous best, that is to say, at its Whitmanian loudest. When Honig heard a fisherman in the Algarve reciting poetry that turned out to be Pessoa's (poetry Honig had never heard before), he did not realize immediately that an American poet's dream—Whitman's—had been fulfilled. As a hopeful Whitmanian poet himself, Honig had carried a copy of the American bard's poetry with him during World War II, part of which he spent in the European theater. Yet Honig was well aware that Whitman, who wished to write for the democratic masses (though he did caution that great poems called for greatness in their audiences), never realized his dream of being read by the people. He did not succeed in becoming a popular poet; rather he depended for his readership on other poets and literature-classes down through the decades. But here, in Portugal, in a small fishing-village bar, his dream came to fruition: here was a "commoner" reciting great poetry. No matter that the fishing village was also a resort town and that, fortunately for Honig, also present in that bar was António Quadros, who besides being a Pessoa scholar was the son of António Ferro, a member of Fernando Pessoa's cohort of writers, artists, and poets of the days of *Orpheu*. According to Honig, it was Quadros who identified the poetry recited by this now forever anonymous fisherman and who introduced him to poetry that, from that moment onward, would play an ever increasing role in Honig's life and work. After recognizing Whitman's language and spirit in the Portuguese poet, Honig embarked on a quest that has not reached its conclusion after four books of translation.

In 1971 Edwin Honig published his translation of Álvaro de Campos's "Ode marítima," which he calls "probably Pessoa's most powerful poem."[3] It appeared in *ND: New Directions 23*, along with the following translator's note:

Fernando Pessoa, Portugal's greatest poet since Camões, was born on June 13, 1888, in Lisbon, and died there on November 30, 1935, practically unknown and unpublished. His poetic works were divided among four heteronyms, or personae: Ricardo Reis, a classicist poet, Alberto Caeiro, a primitive sage and antipoet, Álvaro de Campos, a futurist, and Pessoa himself, writing in both Portuguese and English. . . .

"Maritime Ode" was first published in the second (and final) issue of the *avant-garde* magazine *Orpheu*, in June of 1915. The author, Álvaro de Campos, as imaginary as his literary master, Alberto Caeiro, but also as real as his creator, Fernando Pessoa, is a neurotic disciple of Marinetti and Whitman. A marine engineer trained in Glasgow, de Campos lives in semiretirement in Lisbon and has no idea what or whom to believe in, completely cut off from the past as well as the present.[4]

It is Thomas Merton, whose translations of Pessoa's poems had preceded Honig's translations by four years in the pages of the New Directions annual, that Honig echoes when he calls Alberto Caeiro an "antipoet."[5]

In 1971, Honig also published *Selected Poems by Fernando Pessoa*. In his "Preface: A Note on the Translations," Honig acknowledged that "the late Thomas Merton" had been "an unexpected source of encouragement." "After publishing his group of 'Twelve Poems by Alberto Caeiro' in *New Directions Annual 19*," wrote Honig, "he [Merton] answered my letter, asking what other Pessoa poems he had translated, with the information that he would do no others and had mainly done the dozen to convince Suzuki that Pessoa had really created a Zen Buddhist in the heteronymic poet, Caeiro."[6] Honig also acknowledged the help of "Pessoa's first literary English translator, the American poet and polymath, Edouard Roditi."[7] Soon Honig would have the opportunity to bask in the light of a handsome Keatsian tribute from his fellow poet Karl Shapiro, who sent him a poem, "On First Looking into Honig's Pessoa," which reads:

> This man was three or five or many poets,
> All with their own names, all with their own lives,
> Writing in Portuguese and broken English sonnets,
> A pagan, a parnassian, a herder,
> And that which poetry is all about,
> The metaphysician sick of metaphysics,
> *Solemn investigator of useless things.*
> Fernando Pessoa, as you saluted Whitman
> With one hand tied behind your back,
> I salute you, Honig, and Octavio Paz.[8]

The reference to Paz acknowledges the Mexican poet's seminal essay on Pessoa, "El desconocido de sí mismo," first published in 1961 as the introduction to an edition in Spanish translation of Pessoa's work and reprinted in Edwin Honig's translation as the introduction to his *Selected Poems by Fernando Pessoa* (1971).[9]

In succeeding decades Honig added considerably to his translations of Pessoa. In 1985 appeared *The Keeper of Sheep,* his and Susan M. Brown's translation of Alberto Caeiro's *O guardador de rebanhos* and, a year later, his and Brown's substantial anthology *Poems of Fernando Pessoa.* In 1988, Lawrence Ferlinghetti's City Lights Books brought out *Always Astonished: Selected Prose* by Fernando Pessoa, a volume edited, translated, and introduced by Honig.

What is of immediate interest is not the dissemination of Pessoa's work through Honig's translations but rather how Pessoa's poetry influenced Honig's. Given that Honig dates his acquaintance with Pessoa's poetry from 1963, it is unsurprising that his own poetry was influenced by the work of the Portuguese poet.[10] Thus, as Honig wrote in 1985, it was "through the translations" of Pessoa that "I saw the possibilities of using a variety of voices to carry to completion a long work of my own."[11] That work was *Four Springs,* a book-length poem published in 1972, the year following the publication of his first Pessoa translations.

But specific evidence of how *Four Springs* was influenced by Pessoa's poetry is a rather elusive matter, Honig's own assertion being the strongest evidence there is. Fortunately, the evidence for Pessoa's influence on Honig's poetry is more readily demonstrable in some later poems. In this regard I would single out "Passes for Nicanor Parra," a poem addressed to another of Thomas Merton's antipoets (the other one being Alberto Caeiro); the slippery "Being Somebody"; and, something of a summary performance on the matter of Honig's Pessoa, the more recent poem "Pessoa's Last Masquerade."

In "Passes for Nicanor Parra" one need read only these lines to recall Pessoa (an imperfect anagram for "passes"):

> Evidence piles up day by day
> we do not live
> where we are living
>
> We refurbish   Add a wing
> Rearrange the bed   And
> houses eat us as we sleep.[12]

As for Honig's poem "Being Somebody," the title links it to Campos's "Tabacaria" ("Tobacco Shop"). In his introduction to *Always Astonished,* Honig quotes from his translation of the opening lines of Pessoa's "best-known poem":

> I'm nothing,
> I'll always be nothing.
> I can't even wish to be something.
> Aside from that, I've got all the world's
>   dreams inside me.[13]

Honig's poem "Being Somebody" offers us a narrative analysis of what he imagines to be Pessoa's frustrated reaction to his own heteronymic devices. Caeiro, Reis, Campos—even Pessoa himself—were devices for being someone or, at least, being someone else. To get at this Pessoan core of subdued anguish, Honig adopts a stance that would not be alien to a dying Kierkagaard or the inside-out Thoreau Melville spooked out in the character of Bartleby the scrivener.

> He had need of a way
> to be himself
> without being himself.
>
> He had so little need
> of those who said
> they had need of him,
>
> He wanted never to see
> any of them again,
> though he wouldn't say so.
>
> For once in his life
> he was satisfied
> simply to be.
>
> To be nobody,
> nobody but himself,
> himself without himself.
>
> He felt empty and full—
> not one or the other
> but both at once.

He felt chafed like a child
full of flouting wishes,
flouting elations.

But drained of hankerings
like a glass of water
a thirsty man just drank.

He considered someone odd
though familiar may have come
to live inside of him.

Maybe it meant
he was sheltering someone
who needed a home.

He himself had no home,
flitting from friend
to cousin to stranger,

As the occasion demanded,
or urged by the heart,
which he often misread.

He lived everywhere
but at home, where sometimes
he stayed overnight.

Anywhere he slept
he was at home,
if he didn't overstay.

The city he wished most
to live in was nearby
but quite far away.

Near enough to visit
or be visited by
old friends and children,

Far enough off
to forget them all
in a week or a year.

He wanted to live alone
in a den-like apartment,
working nights on his thoughts,

Or in a big rambling house
without tenants and close
to the hub of the city.

He would like also not
to live there but still
to call it his home

Where he could drop in,
surprising himself hard
at work in his study

Or, having been called away,
finding the place
shrieking his absence.

He'd like to live there
and in the country as well,
unknown except for

The gas-meter reader
who'd fade in and
fade out bimonthly.

He once wrote a letter he thought
he'd only half written himself
which ended limply,

"How many empties like me
are there left to pick up
before I die?"

Now he believed the letter
was written completely
by somebody else.

Of course he was wrong—
but what if he was
completely somebody else?[14]

Tellingly enough, what Honig says about the opening lines of "Tabacaria" applies even more directly to his own poem: "As the exclusively prose-writing semiheteronym Bernardo Soares puts it, 'In each of us there is a differingness and a manyness and a profusion of ourselves.'"[15] This poem is about the different selves of the self. It tells of homes that are not homes (recall, in "Passes for Nicanor Parra," those "houses [that] eat us as we sleep"), of houses in which we would not live but which we call our homes, "den-like apartment[s]" where the poet, living alone, can "work . . . nights on his thoughts," places where the poet meets a surrogate of the poet who insisted that his home-land was the Portuguese language.

"Pessoa was the third literary figure to move me deeply," ac-knowledged Honig in an interview in 1977. "The first was Hart Crane, whom I identified with the hard life of growing up in New York in the thirties and whom I devoured at fourteen and never outgrew. The second was Federico García Lorca whom I latched onto when I was about twenty . . . But Pessoa came to me much later, when in the sixties I gave a course in the theory of literary persona in poetry. Pessoa had to be included along with Wallace Stevens, Rilke, and Pound."[16] He might well have included in this list William Butler Yeats, whom Jorge de Sena has called Pessoa's only rival among the Anglo-Saxon poets of modernism.[17]

In 1988, at the Lisbon meetings celebrating the Pessoa cen-tenary, Honig began his talk with a reference to Yeats. "In his elegy on the Irish poet W.B. Yeats, W.H. Auden wrote, 'The death of the poet was kept from his poems'; and, 'he became his admirers.'" Honig continued, "Our being here today testifies to a similar fact about Pessoa: 'The words of a dead man / are mod-ified in the guts of the living.' For like the words of Yeats and other poets, Pessoa in all he wrote will be transformed in a process of cultural crosspollination."[18] At the end of his brief talk Honig offered his audience some lines "in homage to 'meu mestre,' Caeiro-Reis-de-Campos-Pessoa."[19] The title of the poem, "Pessoa's Last Masquerade," echoes the subtitle of Mel-ville's last novel *The Confidence-Man* and exemplifies perfectly the cultural cross-pollination that he was talking about. To be kept in mind are some of Honig's own notions, as expressed in his *Dark Conceit* (1959), regarding Melville's confidence-man:

A paragon of Christian charity who makes fraudulence profitable in the various guises of an impostor, he seems gradually to victimize himself. . . .

Each disguise of the Confidence Man hints at a previous role he has played and foreshadows a new one he will shortly undertake. . . . This situation [in Kafka] is another version of the problem dealt with in *The Confidence Man*—that of having somehow to support the illusion against the reality: untenable though the illusion may be, there is no alternative. For the positive world endures against the proof of its own irrationality, which is shown in the failure of the hero.[20]

Such are the Melvillean notions packed into the poem Honig entitled "Pessoa's Last Masquerade":

> "Be admitted to the heart of your own
>   self
> dismissal," he proposed, choking on the effort
>   to waken
> the hidden one, the only shifter he kept
>   subtracting,
> more vehement, more drastic and diminished
>   each day
> than he'd admit. (Admit? To whom? His self-
>   lessness?
> The real self was his tool for scrutiny.)
>   Lashed,
> it cried, "Admit, admit!" but this he could
>   not bear.
>
> The shifter, now colliding with him, spat out:
>   "Who are
> *you* if not myself?" "Yourself," he crowed,
>   "therefore
> a friend?" "Be nothing," it snapped at him
>   again.
> "Be yourself in silence but something less than
>   a friend.
> Be anything not your own, no selfless self-
>   prolonger.
> Practice a face for life's sake but be some-
>   one else!"
>
> A day to reckon with—he'd roused the last one
>   just

to give it life and with this start something
    new:
the opening to let them . . . let out all
    the self
shifters fed daily on his remorseless words.
    Happening
so swiftly, so it passed, the last one
    to drift
way down through some pinpoint hole
    growing
in the remembered dark until he felt them all
    sucked in.

Then, with nothing to elude, nothing to feed
    in him,
the absence began—an absence, he saw, of all-
    become-him:
the one who might be, the one who was, the someone
    unborn
or long dead and never to come at him
    again.
Enemy friend admitted it, waking only
    for that,
with no words to forgive, as if even
    so little
were too much to give his briefly final
    being.[21]

This poem is also reminiscent of Roditi, who in 1955 had called attention to Pessoa's interest in the "theme of the mask or person."[22] Honig invokes Yeats's notion of the poetic mask to give us a poetic take on Pessoa's dilemma when he saw himself facing his final days alone—sans heteronyms. Alberto Caeiro, long since dead, no longer inspired the writing even of predated poems, and Ricardo Reis, still presumably alive, had now disappeared seemingly irrevocably into the dim distance of far-off Brazilian life. It was true that Álvaro de Campos was still with him and would stay to the end, but the retired naval engineer had his own somewhat unpredictable agenda and could not always be counted on for the kind of company Pessoa needed. Campos was having his own difficulties with identity. He too had once tried to remove the ineffectual mask he had assumed but found it difficult to do so:

The domino I put on was wrong.
They knew me right off for someone I was not and I did not disabuse
    them, but lost myself.
When I tried to pull off the mask
It stuck to my face.
When I got it off and saw myself in the mirror,
I had aged.
I was drunk and knew no longer how to wear the domino I had not
    removed.[23]

Finally, as recorded in a late poem the author dated August 18, 1934, Campos succeeded in removing the mask. The result was not what he had expected.

I set aside the mask and looked in the mirror.
It was the child of so many years ago
It had not changed at all.
Nothing at all had changed.

That's the edge in knowing how to remove the mask.
One is always the child,
The past that remains,
The child.

I set aside the mask and then replaced it.
That's better.
That way I am the mask.

And I return to what's normal as if it were the last station at the end
    of a line.[24]

But the day finally arrived when the orthonymic Pessoa himself found himself before that ultimate opportunity to face the true self so long avoided on account of his heteronyms, including the self who also wrote poems and other things. The unknown beast within himself, whose responses might not be in accord with what he wanted at all, calls up this center-of-the-onion "enemy friend"—"the one whose very self was hidden from him," as Octavio Paz had so perceptively described Pessoa a quarter of a century after his death.[25] All other heteronyms "drift way down through some pinpoint hole" that this Alice will enter, preferring to face the beast of himself—this "briefly final being." Of course, even this encounter is a masquerade, as the poet has assumed one final mask—the mask of the adventurer dropping down into the self to discover his true being. Does Honig's masquerader get there, does he strike through that mask to his authentic, sincere self? Or has the old artificer of necessity pulled off once again that piece of legerdemain he so succinctly acknowledged practicing in one of his English sonnets?

> How many masks wear we, and undermasks,
> Upon our countenance of soul, and when,
> If for self-sport the soul itself unmasks,
> Knows it the last mask off and the face plain?
> The true mask feels no inside to the mask
> But looks out of the mask by co-masked eyes.
> Whatever consciousness begins the task
> The task's accepted use to dulness ties.
> Like a child frighted by its mirrored faces,
> Our souls, that children are, being thought-losing,
> Foist otherness upon their seen grimaces
> And get a whole world on their forgot causing;
>   And, when a thought would unmask our soul's masking,
>   Itself goes not unmasked to the unmasking.[26]

This sonnet was published in 1918. Three years earlier Pessoa's *Orpheu* collaborator, the Brazilian poet Ronald de Carvalho, had inscribed a sketch of his likeness "To Fernando Pessoa, exquisite sculptor of masks."[27]

Yeats's first prominent use of the concept of the mask dates from the same period. In 1910 he included a song entitled "The Mask" in *The Player Queen*. The poem is a precursor of Honig's "Pessoa's Last Masquerade," which in itself combines Pessoa's preoccupation with masks (and heteronymity) with both Yeats's similar preoccupations and his employment of direct address. Yeats's poem begins:

"Put off that mask of burning gold
With emerald eyes."
"O no, my dear, you make so bold
To find if hearts be wild and wise,
And yet not cold."

"I would but find what's there to find,
Love or deceit."
"It was the mask engaged your mind,
And after set your heart to beat,
Not what's behind."

Although we cannot be certain Pessoa knew this Yeats poem or
that he was even aware of Yeats's preoccupation with the concept of the poetic mask, it is certain that he knew something of
Yeats's early work. In 1917, to the first and only issue of *Portugal
Futurista*, Álvaro de Campos had contributed his "Ultimatum,"
in which he banished the Irish poet: "Out with you, Yeats, you,
with your Celtic haze circling an unmarked post, a sack of rot-
tenness washed ashore from the shipwreck of English symbol-
ism."[28] The mask was a different matter. There, as Honig tacitly
acknowledges, Pessoa could out-Yeats Yeats, recognizing, with
a bit more irony than Yeats, that, as Nietzsche says, "Profundity,
loves the mask"—or something, at least, that countenances profundity. Pessoa has Álvaro de Campos conclude a prose contribution to *Presença* in 1927, "To pretend is to know oneself."[29]
Yeats puts it another way: "Seeming that goes on for a lifetime
is no different from reality."[30]

As for Honig's knowing self-knowledge, it might not have
been entirely a *blague* when, under Dutch attack for his first
translations of Pessoa, he donned his Yeatsian-Pessoan mask
and revealed himself as Fernando's "latest heteronym."[31]

5

City Lights

Lawrence Ferlinghetti

The bare bones are these. In 1922 a Portuguese poet publishes a story, which, five and a half decades later, is translated into French. The French version catches the eye of an American poet who has discovered that he has Portuguese ancestors. The American then writes a novella that is heavily indebted to the Portuguese story. Later the American, who is also a publisher, engages a third poet to undertake the task of turning the Portuguese story into English, translating it not from the French version that the publisher-poet had admired but from the original Portuguese. Thereby hangs a tale.

Lawrence Ferlinghetti's fame as a Beat Generation writer—largely established by his early book *A Coney Island of the Mind*, which has sold over a million copies—continues to obscure the fact that for over fifty years he has pursued a double career as an experimental writer and as a highly influential publisher. Since the early 1950s he has been the proprietor of City Lights Bookstore, which he cofounded, and the director of City Lights Books, founded at the same time.

It was as both writer and publisher that Ferlinghetti first encountered the work of Fernando Pessoa, a discovery that might have been related to his own discoveries about his own Portuguese ancestry. Ferlinghetti was already an adult when he learned that his maternal grandfather was one Herman Mendes-Monsanto, the son of a broker whose family (descended from Sephardim Jews originally from the village of Monsanto) had settled on the Caribbean island of St. Thomas after emigrating from Portugal.[1] Herman's daughter Clemence met her future husband, Carlo Ferlinghetti, at Coney Island in the 1890s, but Lawrence was not born until 1919, and then he was not raised by his parents. The story of his unconventional upbringing, carried out largely by strangers, falls outside the scope of my book, but suffice it to say that Ferlinghetti learned the basic facts of his heritage rather late and then not in their entirety. There are no appreciable references to Portuguese history or literature in his work before 1988, when, in his seventieth year, this child of an Italian father and a Portuguese-Jewish mother published *Love in the Days of Rage*, a novella set in Paris during the 1968 student uprisings.

Ferlinghetti spent some of his childhood in France and had returned in the 1940s to study at the University of Paris, where he earned a doctorate in 1949. When he returned to Paris in the summer of 1985, Ferlinghetti did so to paint. But he ended up doing something else. "I kept running into people I had known in Paris in '68," he said, "which started me thinking about the novel [*Love in the Days of Rage*]. Then I really got wrapped up in research on it. I went to the Musée de Pompidou where they have a big library of periodicals, and I could look up on microfilm all the French periodicals for the student revolution of '68. So I spent all this time reading issues of the newspapers and magazines of that time from January '68 through that summer."[2] At first Ferlinghetti tried to write his novel in French but found it difficult to sustain the language when he got down, as he said, to the nitty-gritty. He then turned to English, and after a false narrative start—in which he told the story from the first-person-singular point of view of a woman—he completed his novella using the third person singular. Ferlinghetti's biographer does not tell us when Pessoa entered into his subject's thinking about his love-and-rage novel. Yet one may suspect that, ever the wary philosophical anarchist, Ferlinghetti might have had Pessoa in mind from the beginning, for the sociopolitical discourse of Pessoa's 1922 tale pervades the text of *Love in the Days of Rage*. Ferlinghetti acknowledges his literary debt by dedicating his book to "Fernando Pessoa whose Anarchist Banker," he allows, "prefigured" his own.[3]

Handsome as it is, this dedication is potentially misleading, for the notion of prefiguration fails to convey adequately the nature and extent of the American writer's indebtedness to the

Portuguese modernist poet. The relationship between Pessoa's "O banqueiro anarquista" and Ferlinghetti's novella is far more direct and familial, for the character whom Ferlinghetti calls Julian Mendes, a Portuguese native working as a banker in Paris, reinvents, at times in detail, the political and economic notions of Pessoa's wonderfully complacent anarchist.[4] We need not rehearse the details of Pessoa's unnamed banker's apologia for his astonishingly coherent stance as a truly practical theorist of anarchism to see that the Portuguese banker in the Paris of 1968 has shamelessly (and without any acknowledgment or, perhaps, knowledge) taken over the arguments of Pessoa's anarchist. It might be interesting to know just when Ferlinghetti encountered Pessoa's "O banqueiro anarquista" and in what language. He did not need to read it in the original Portuguese, for by 1978 the novella was available in French translation.[5] There was no English translation until, years later, Ferlinghetti himself commissioned one.

Undoubtedly, Pessoa's story appealed to Ferlinghetti less as a source of new ideas than as a corroboration of some of his own. There must have been a shock of self-recognition in the self-portrait given by Pessoa's anarchist banker, who insists that he is an anarchist who happens to be a banker and not a banker who happens to be an anarchist. After all, Ferlinghetti sometimes characterizes himself as an anarchist-artist who happens to be a bookseller and publisher. In Pessoa's tale Ferlinghetti not only discovered a text that he could rewrite to suit himself, but in Pessoa's banker he might also have discovered an alter ego, a somewhat exaggerated version of himself not as anarchist-artist but as anarchist-businessman.

In choosing to name his San Francisco project "City Lights," Ferlinghetti was undoubtedly paying tribute to Paris. It might be a living reminder to him of his early, personal, and perdurable affection for the City of Light. Modeled on French examples, the City Lights venture was to be from the start both a capitalist pursuit—selling books at a profit—and an artistic journey—publishing poetry and literature that was in accord with his own aesthetic and political ideals. His bookstore would recreate in the New World what he admired about the City of Light. In this way he would earn his living in the midst of an

American bourgeois world and continue to work toward effecting change in that world through the creation, propagation, and dissemination of literature that might subvert that world. That he early on acquired a publisher—New Directions—for his own work, a publisher whose mission was avowedly more aesthetic and cultural than political, did not compromise his ideals or betray his intentions. On the contrary, giving his work a "safe" home in the relatively comfortable world of letters that New Directions provided for him (its reputation for promoting the lesser commercial lights of modernism and the safer works of the avant-garde did not hurt in this) enabled him to publish with seemingly greater independence and even "establishment" authority the "revolutionary" literature that suited his long-term political purposes. In short, he devised a modus vivendi that enabled him to stand forth as an independent publisher without compromising his situation as a self-supporting member of his society. Understanding this might help to explain what Ferlinghetti meant when he described himself once as "an anarchist among the floorwalkers."[6]

While Ferlinghetti might have found in Pessoa's portrayal of an anarchist a rough intellectual and political equivalent of himself, he seems to have decided to draw the portrait even more closely in the figure of Julian Mendes. A high official at the Bank of France, Julian bears part of Ferlinghetti's maternal grandfather's Portuguese surname of Mendes-Monsanto. Whereas Pessoa's rather static story is just barely dramatized as an after-dinner conversation (a monologue actually), Ferlinghetti plots out a love story between his banker and Annie, an American artist in Paris, who at the age of forty is fifteen years Mendes's junior, to be played out against the student and worker uprisings in Paris in the spring of 1968. This bit of history enables Ferlinghetti to display his own understanding of how a more modern-day businessman might insist upon being taken seriously as a practical anarchist.

Just as Pessoa's banker must tell his autobiographical story of how he became first an anarchist and then a banker, so too does Ferlinghetti's banker. Just as Pessoa's unnamed protagonist finds the need to explain his anarchist principles in order to justify his own view of himself as both a theoretical and a practical anarchist, so too does Julian Mendes resort to the same strategic points in answering his lover's skeptical questions regarding what she finds to be the obvious disparities in what Mendes purports to believe and the way he has chosen to live his life.

"What is an anarchist?" asks Pessoa's banker. "He's a rebel against the injustice of being born *socially* unequal," he answers.[7] His aim is to establish a "free society" by means of "an intense, complete, all-engulfing propaganda" that will "predispose all spirits and weaken all resistance" to the passage from a bourgeois society to a free society. The banker explains that by "propaganda" he does not mean "simply the spoken and written word." He means "everything: direct and indirect action, whatever can promote the free society and weaken any opposition to its advent." The result will be that, "having scarcely any resistance to overcome, the social revolution, when it arrives, will be swift and easy and will not have to set up a revolutionary dictatorship, having nobody against whom to apply it" (87). But what does an anarchist want? "He wants to be free, from the time he's born and appears in the world, as he justly ought to be; and he wants such freedom for himself and for everybody else" (89).

There is a catch. Nature does not make everyone equal. "Some are born tall, others not; some strong, others weak; some more intelligent, others less so," though in every other way human beings can be equal. What prevents that equality are the "social myths," which must be destroyed (89). Yet social equality is difficult to achieve, for some men "imperceptibly become leaders," while others "imperceptibly become underlings." The anarchist banker explains with an example:

Some became bosses by main force, others by ruse. This was apparent in the smallest matters. For example: Two fellows were going down a street together; they came to the end of the block and one had to go to the right and the other to the left; each found it convenient to go his own way. But the one going to the left said to the other. "Come on with me this way;" and the other replied—and it was true: "Man, I can't; I've got to go that way"—for one reason or another . . . . But in the end, against his own will and interest, he nevertheless went to the left with the other. . . . This occurred once through persuasion, another time through simple insistence, a third time through some motive of a similar kind . . . . It was never for any logical reason, and always in the domination and subordination there was something spontaneous as there was something instinctive. [94]

The result is that in the "present social setup," there is no possibility for effective collaborative action in groups of men, "however well intentioned they all may be, however dedicated they all are in fighting social myths and in working for liberty, to work together without spontaneously creating tyranny among themselves, without creating among them a new tyranny to supplement the social myths, without in practice destroying all that they wish for in theory, without involuntarily upsetting entirely the very purpose they wish to promote." What must be done is "very simple," answers the banker. Men must work for the same end but do so "separately" (98).

Working separately in this way and for the same anarchist goal, we have two advantages: that of a common effort, and that of not creating a new tyranny. We remain united, because we are morally bound and because we work in the same manner toward the same goal. We remain anarchists because each one works for the free society, but we cease to betray our cause, consciously or unconsciously; we also cease to be able to do so, because we place ourselves, by virtue of working for anarchism individually, outside of the deleterious influence of the social myths with their inherited reflexes upon the qualities that Nature endows.

It's clear that such a strategy pertains to what I call the *period of preparation* for the social revolution. Once the bourgeois defenses lie in ruin and their whole society is reduced to accepting the doctrines of the anarchists, the only thing to accomplish then is the final blow, with the period of isolated action no longer possible to continue. For by then the free society will have virtually arrived; the state of things will have changed. The strategy I referred to only obtains to anarchist action in a bourgeois milieu, as it was with the group I belonged to. [99]

Thus it is that humanity must be prepared for the advent of a free society through "indirect action, that is, through propaganda, and direct action of whatever kind" (101).

Yet the banker insists that an individual cannot destroy social myths, that only a revolution can, though an individual can subjugate a social myth. And in his time, he insists, the most important of those social myths is money. The question then is simply one of learning how to free oneself from the influence and power of money. In a parody of Alberto Caeiro's naturalist's argument, the banker rejects the "simplest procedure," which is to withdraw from society, to remove himself "from its sphere of influence, that is, from civilization; go off to the country, eat roots, and drink water out of springs; go around naked and live like an animal." That will not work. "[It] would not be fighting a social myth; it wouldn't even be fighting, it would be escaping. It's true that to avoid engaging in combat is not to be overcome by it. Yet it is being morally vanquished because it means not having fought. The procedure would be of that sort: It would involve combat and not the avoidance of combat. How to subjugate money by fighting it? How to divest oneself of its influence and tyranny without avoiding the need to meet it head on?" The answer is simple. "There was only one way: *to acquire it,* acquire it in sufficient quantity to feel its influence no longer, and the more one acquired, the freer one would be from its influence" (104).

Only when the would-be anarchist sees this clearly, with all the power of his convictions as an anarchist and with all his logic as a lucid being, can he embark on "the real phase—namely, the mercantile and banking phase" of his anarchism (104). And the process will work, for "in growing superior to the power of money," argues the banker, he will gain *liberty* for himself. If he cannot, working alone, achieve liberty for all—social myths can only be destroyed by revolution—he can nevertheless take this crucial first step (105). For this banker is unlike those anarchists who are only anarchists in theory. "They are anarchist mystics"; while he, "a scientific anarchist," is an anarchist "in theory and in practice" (109).

The major way in which Ferlinghetti's banker differs from Pessoa's makes all the difference. "I am waiting / for the war to be fought / which will make the world safe / for anarchy," the words Ferlinghetti had once written in a poem, could be those of his banker in Paris in 1968.[8] As if looking back to his own anarchist's high hopes in Paris that spring at a moment when many seemed to feel that anarchist "propaganda" had finally germinated and produced genuine revolution, the author of

Love in the Days of Rage writes elegiacally of the events that began with such high revolutionary promise and ended so badly. Pessoa's anarchist banker had acknowledged that the strategy of working "individually" pertains only to "the *period of preparation* for the social revolution." For "once the bourgeois defenses lie in ruin and their whole society is reduced to accepting the doctrines of the anarchists," he explains, "the only thing to accomplish then is the final blow, with the period of isolated action no longer possible to continue" (99). Individual work directed at the destruction of social myths, having contributed to the overall work of destructive propaganda, will then be abandoned before the greater need to deliver that final blow. Pessoa's banker never explains what that final, collaborative blow might be or how, when the time comes, an individual might be called upon to participate in its delivery. Ferlinghetti's banker, however, finds himself at that moment in history when he feels called upon to strike that very blow. When his lover asks him, in the midst of the "revolution" that each of them feels sure is unfolding before their very eyes, if he will now abandon what she takes to be his hypocritical strategy of individual action in favor of striking the blow that will benefit everyone, he finally recognizes that history has put him on the spot. "According to your so-called anarchist principles, isn't this *the* famous time of insurrection you're always talking about," she asks, "the exact moment you've finally got to act, the very moment you've been waiting for? Isn't this *the* moment when you'll finally have to give up 'acting alone' and act with everyone else to bring about the real takeover?" (82-83). He hesitates, mulling things over, procrastinates, points to a natural symbol of tyranny in the interaction of two small birds, then decides. "It is the time, and it could really happen this time" (83). His plan, he reveals, is to blow up that section of the train carrying "a very large part of the Bank of France's most valuable stuff" to safety in "a secret vault out in the country" (84).

Sixty years after its initial publication, "O banqueiro anarquista" was reissued in Lisbon. Accompanying Pessoa's text was an introductory essay, "Fernando Pessoa, O mito e a realidade," signed "K., *Sine Nomine Vulgus.*" The motives behind the republication of Pessoa's story are subversive, as K., who signs out of Brussels, makes painfully obvious: "Fernando Pessoa in Portugal, and even in other geographical spaces, was . . . incapable of understanding the world in which he lived or—above all—the possibility of that world's being subverted."[9] In fact, "an individual-man can never exist," he editorializes, for "either we are a collective of individuals experiencing those shared passions that are the fruit of the desire of each of us, or we are condemned forever to the sadness of the Pessoas and their banal writings."[10] Calling him "a poet who does not know what Poetry is," K. would hoist Pessoa on his own petard by applying to him the paradox about poetry, reworked in political terms, that the poet had presented in the poem "Autopsicografia": "[Pessoa] fakes things so completely that he even fakes that they are reactionary, those reactionary feelings that he truly feels."[11]

Oddly, "O banqueiro anarquista" has not been much explored by those readers looking for evidence of Pessoa's own political ideas.[12] Pessoa's editors, with a great deal of nonfictional political material available to them, are usually satisfied to pigeonhole "O banqueiro anarquista" as one of his so-called "reasoning" tales, discouraging thereby those readers who might otherwise see in it a locus for Pessoa's own political ideas. Yet Pessoa's fiction, which is usually short on characterization—"O banqueiro anarquista" is no exception—is long on ideas and concepts. It does make sense, of course, to regard the text as a fictional work of some narrative complexity. Although the bulk of the narrative consists of a long statement by the unnamed banker, in which he explains his origins and how he continues to be a true anarchist, his statement is contained within the retrospective narrative by the banker's unnamed acquaintance. The banker proceeds logically through an argument that is intended to demonstrate that he is a true anarchist in idea and practice. Several questions can be honestly asked. Does the banker speak sincerely and forthrightly? Does he believe that what he is and what he does make him an authentic anarchist? Is he being deliberately deceitful, using a travesty of logic and shameless sophistry to validate his own capitalistic greed? Is he merely showing off his ability to turn thoughts inside out, to make them mean their opposite and worse? Is this cigar-smoking anarchist merely blowing smoke to deceive his inquisitive dinner companion? Is the author's intention to undercut all arguments favoring a form of anarchism that goes beyond talk and bombs? Does he endorse the banker's view that anarchism means freedom and that only the individual can achieve freedom? Does control over money, once it has been secured, lead to the achievement of individual freedom, as the banker argues? In short, what is the author's stance toward the banker's ideas and practice?

Love in the Days of Rage ends inconclusively with Julian's lover standing in the wilds of western France, at or beyond the Spanish border, awaiting the arrival of Julian, who has told her only that the bomb he is carrying will be used to blow up the train carrying the key materials of the Bank of France to a secret place secure from the incursions of the worker-student revolution spreading through France. Destroying this train, he implies, will, in effect, destroy the very basis for the bourgeois system of the French government itself. But we do not know that Julian will join Annie (who has been guided to their meeting place by Caiero, Julian's friend with the misapplied and misspelled Pessoan name); we do not know even whether he intends to do so; whether he survives the bombing of the train; whether he does set off the bomb; whether he truly intends to blow up the train or is merely blowing off Annie with his story; whether he really does have a bomb he can carry aboard the train; whether he really does consider himself an anarchist; and so on. The reader of course lacks the information to determine the author's own attitude toward the ideas about anarchism that are espoused by his banker.

Besides taking over Pessoa's principal—the anarchist banker himself—Ferlinghetti borrows Pessoa's banker's arguments about personal freedom and theoretical and practical anarchism. Distinguishing between natural inequality among men (about which nothing can be done) and the social inequality that emerges among them (which can potentially be eradicated), Ferlinghetti's banker decides that the state must always be opposed, because all governments are oppressive. To oppose social conventions successfully, one must recognize that, however customary they have become, they are artificial. Unrecognized as such, these habits become the source of the tyranny that men exercise over other men whenever they try to work together.

If someone said Go Right here, and another said Go Left, we went in the direction of the one who seemed to know best, et cetera. But the bigger our underground network became, the more power our leaders had over everyone in the underground. So we were creating our own set of controls, claiming they were necessary just temporarily—just a little temporary exercise of power over the others, for the common good, of course. The trouble is that the supposedly temporary police power never somehow "withers away" as it is supposed to. [62-63]

The key to the practice of anarchism, as Ferlinghetti's banker recognizes, is that men must work toward freedom, but they must do so separately:

Work for the same ends, but work separately! Yes, that was it, that was it exactly. Working separately we'd all be separately free. And acting separately had the advantage of complete secrecy, which we couldn't have in a group. Of course I realized that this could only work during the early stages and that the final "coup" could only be accomplished by acting together. But we were a long way from that! [63]

He tells us that he tried out his new ideas on his fellow anarchists, but they rejected them and chastised him. So he put his ideas into practice by "joining" the banking system:

I was out to beat the evil system, as I conceived it, with all its dirty practices, and I should quibble about my methods? I was working toward freedom from the whole wicked mess, and I should be more critical as to what arms I use to attack? The idiot anarchist with his spiteful little bombs in the street firing at random knows damn well he's going to kill people even though his anarchist theories exclude capital punishment. He's violating his principles but he's right morally because he expects his violent act will make the future better, and I wanted to beat repression and poverty and establish a perfect state, and for that I used any means I could get hold of, without of course creating any *new* evils. Well, I freed myself from the system, by grasping the root of it, money! Having conquered the root of evil, I freed myself. [66-67]

Does this speech provide the evidence to unmask a fraudulent banker who claims to be an anarchist or to recognize in him a practical anarchist who becomes a banker so that he can realize the potential of his theories by putting them into action?

The year 1922, in which Pessoa published "O banqueiro anarquista," saw republican Portugal in its customary political turmoil, with governments tumbling, one after the other, like tenpins. Before the decade was out, however, Portugal's twenty-some-year experiment with democratic republicanism, although not widely perceived as such, had effectively ended and would not return for the next half century. A military takeover in 1928, seen as an interregnum, turned out to be that only in the sense that the military dictatorship would soon give way to a budding fascist dictatorship headed by António Salazar, an economist recruited from the faculty of the University of Coimbra. That the scaffolding for the *Estado Novo* (New State), as it would be called, was already in place and that the edifice itself would last for nearly five decades, was apparent to no one. In fact, there is some evidence that Pessoa at first, like most of the Portuguese, welcomed the newly established political and economic orderliness that Dr. Salazar and his regime brought to the nation. But Pessoa's approval of the New State would not last. Early in 1935 he wrote a strong defense of "secret societies," particularly the Masonic orders, which were under direct attack. He intended to publish that defense anonymously but it ended up appearing over his signature. That summer, just months before his death, he wrote satirical poems about the character of Salazar and the New State, doggerel that he knew could not be published while Salazar ran the country. One of those poems, lacking a line in the final stanza, is a mock-elegy for the Portuguese people living in the New State:

> Portugal, my poor Portugal,
> My heart aches for you.
> What befalls you befalls me
> In my imaginary.

> Frail, sickly,
> Showing that superficial
> Flush that consumption
> Brings to the face.

> My people, poor and thin,
> Given the pieces to a

New outfit so that
You will look the part.

Face scrubbed,
Outfitted for show,
But given nothing,
Poor thing, to eat.

And there you sit,
Dazed, presentable.

An amiable transient.[13]

Salazar does not figure in Pessoa's tale of anarchism. His banker achieved the reality of print a good five years before Dr. Salazar appeared on the national scene. Writing in the 1980s, Ferlinghetti has the opportunity to bring into his tale of 1968 "news" of Salazar's then seemingly interminable regime as well as that of other European fascist regimes. His banker discusses his idea of anarchism against the backdrop of Salazar's fascism. "What kind of antifascism were we working for anyway?" the Portuguese-French banker asks, knowing the answer:

The reason the state ends up victimizing people is because the state crystallizes all our social conventions—and those conventions themselves are all false—they're not natural laws, they're acquired. Like carrying guns . . . . We are not born carrying guns, we're not born in police uniforms, we're not born wearing gas masks and carrying riot sticks—it's a habit which has grown upon us, so that it almost seems natural, and then it becomes "natural" to kill each other with guns in the name of law and order and common sense, and so then it becomes perfectly natural for us to kill each other *en masse* periodically, to preserve law and order, to protect our property, our group, our gang, our nation, our tribe, or whatever. Property itself is not something natural we come out of the womb with but it begins to *look* like it's natural, with the laws we set up to pass it on. [59]

Then he turns to a consideration of how the "naturalization" of the laws governing property evolves "naturally" into "natural" governments and their leaders.

And so it becomes natural to govern everyone more and more, for the "greater good," they say—and Franco becomes natural, Mussolini becomes natural, Salazar becomes natural, Hitler becomes natural. So all this enormous structure we have built up is a social *fiction* which ends up tyrannizing us. . . . I knew the only way the system could ever be upset would be by a sudden insurrection. But then the same thing would happen again—another gang would take over and make its own new rules, and they in turn would become institutionalized, and there you would have it again, another monstrous organized lie created out of whole cloth, or whole paper, a whole new paper palace, a whole new house of cards, printed with the latest letterheads of those in power. This time it would be *our* gang, but nevertheless, it would end up the same—[59-60]

Anyone familiar with Pessoa's "O banqueiro anarquista" will readily see that the orderly thinking about anarchism of the banker Julian Mendes closely parallels that of Pessoa's banker, who insists, "The true evil, the only evil, is the conventions and the social myths superimposed on natural realities" (83). As for the references to the twentieth-century Spanish, Italian, German, and Portuguese dictators, consider Pessoa's banker's observations:

What ensues from a revolutionary dictatorship—and will continue more and more to ensue from it—is a combative society of the dictatorial type, that is, military despotism. Nor can it ever be anything else. And it's always been so. . . . What occurred after the political agitations in Rome? The Roman Empire and its military despotism. What happened after the French Revolution? Napoleon and his military despotism. And you'll see what's to come after the Russian revolution: something that will set back the achievement of a free society for decades and decades. [86-87]

Ferlinghetti's original indebtedness to Pessoa in *Love in the Days of Rage* seems to have been greater than even the final version indicates. He was persuaded to delete "some of the anarchist banker's theory conversation, which had been taken directly from the book's model, Fernando Pessoa's *The Anarchist Banker*."[14] James Laughlin, his longtime publisher at New Directions, suggested even more radical cuts. He wanted the

anarchist banker himself replaced by—shades of Ezra Pound—
"a social credit banker."[15] Laughlin failed to see that the combi-
nation of "anarchism" with banking was the key to what
Ferlinghetti wanted from Pessoa's text. It enabled him to or-
chestrate his overall "deep-seated mistrust of all governments
and their incursions on individual freedom."[16] For the first time
Laughlin turned down a Ferlinghetti manuscript.

Pessoa did not reprint "O banqueiro anarquista" after its
first publication in 1922. In 1935, however, he talked of bringing
out an English version of his novella. He told Adolfo Casais Monteiro that he was working on an "entirely remodeled
version" that he would first reprint, and then translate into
English. The story had "European prospects," thought Pessoa,
and he would himself see about getting it published in
England.[17] By return mail, on January 20, Casais Monteiro
suggested that the British writer Richard Aldington might serve
as Pessoa's intermediary in London.[18] But Pessoa replied that he
had in mind someone else who could act on his behalf. "If there
is in the work something that will make it of interest to the
English market," he continued, "the literary agent to whom I
will send it will place it sooner or later."[19] Nothing came of
Pessoa's plans. In less than a year the poet was dead. Only in
1988 did the first English translation of "O banqueiro anarquista" appear, under the imprint of City Lights Books. It was
included in *Always Astonished,* a selection of Pessoa's prose
made by Edwin Honig, who also translated the texts that Pessoa
had not supplied in English. But the original plan, a Ferlinghetti initiative, had called for the publication of only *The Anarchist Banker.*

6

Barbaric Complaint

Allen Ginsberg

In *Walt Whitman: The Measure of His Song,* an anthology of poetic responses (in poetry and prose) to Whitman that was published by Holy Cow! Press in 1981, Allen Ginsberg is represented by two titles, the poem "A Supermarket in California," first published in 1955, and a prose piece called "Allen Ginsberg on Walt Whitman: Composed on the Tongue," which dates from 1980. The latter piece, described as a "Discourse," appears to be a lightly edited transcription of Ginsberg's commentary "on consecutive pages of the Modern Library Edition of *Leaves of Grass* in a sound studio in Boulder, Colorado (1980) for use by Centre Films as a spontaneous sketch of Whitman's works as a sound track for a film."[1]

"There was a man, Walt Whitman, who lived in the nineteenth century, in America," Ginsberg declares, "who began to define his own person, who began to tell his own secrets, who outlined his own body, and made an outline of his own mind, so other people could see it."[2] He feels his way along for a couple of sentences and then says a thing that must seem extraordinary, especially to anyone interested in Ginsberg's reading of Fernando Pessoa:

He began announcing himself, and announcing person, with a big capital P, Person, self, or one's own nature, one's own original nature, what you really think when you're alone in bed, after everybody's gone home from the party or when you're looking in the mirror, shaving, or you're not shaving and you're looking in the mirror, looking at your long, white, aged beard, or if you're sitting on the toilet, or thinking to yourself "What happened to life?" "What happened to your Mommy?" or if you're just walking down the street, looking at people full of longing.[3]

It is as if Ginsberg is already seeing Whitman through the lens supplied by Pessoa, the "Mr. Person" of John Wain's 1979 poem. Furthermore, it is as if he has been influenced by the notion of Pessoa's biographer (João Gaspar Simões), who maintained that Pessoa never recovered from the "loss" of his mother when she remarried after his father's death. It is as if Ginsberg's Whitman, "walking down the street, looking at people full of longing," has been reading the Álvaro de Campos who wrote "Tabacaria" ("Tobacco Shop") or "Cruz na porta" ("Cross on the Door"). Ginsberg has undoubtedly taken his cue from "One's-Self I Sing," the "very first *inscription* [my emphasis; Pessoa also wrote a series of "Inscriptions"—in English], at the beginning of *Leaves of Grass*," that starts out: "One's-Self I sing, a simple separate person."[4]

As luck would have it, Pessoa is also represented in *Walt Whitman: The Measure of His Song*, by Álvaro de Campos's "Salutation to Walt Whitman" (in Edwin Honig's translation). Ed Folsom's introduction observes that Pessoa's poem, written in 1915, preceded the publication of García Lorca's "Ode to Walt Whitman" by fifteen years, thus making Pessoa's poem (after Rubén Darío's sonnet "Walt Whitman" in 1890) the second major "Hispanic" poetic tribute to Whitman. ("Hispanic" is Folsom's term.) Calling it a "passionate" poem, Folsom describes "Saudação a Walt Whitman": "The salutation clamors for openness and 'pressing forward,' and celebrates the 'abandon and joyous mutual possession' and the 'morality of complete freedom' that Lorca too came to see embodied in Whitman. Pessoa claims that Campos is far more than a follower of Whitman, is rather an actual *incarnation* carrying on Walt's sensual release."[5] This claim by Álvaro de Campos, Pessoa's Whitman-like heteronym, that he *is* Walt Whitman is precisely what Ginsberg loudly disputes in his 1988 poem "Salutations to Fernando Pessoa."[6]

Ginsberg was one of the era's most notable practitioners of the public put-on. And it is as the work of a trickster-poet that Ginsberg's apostrophic poem to Pessoa can be best understood, for, read as the deadpan product of the serious and solemn poet, "Salutations to Fernando Pessoa" seems utterly self-serving and downright mean-spirited. One would never guess, if the poem were taken without that saving grain of salt, that Ginsberg the teacher thought well enough of Pessoa (as Edwin Honig testifies) to include translations of his work in his classes.[7]

"Salutations to Fernando Pessoa" takes its title and some of its formal and verbal inspiration not only from Walt Whitman's "Salut au monde" but from "Saudação a Walt Whitman," Pessoa's own tribute (in the voice of his heteronym Álvaro de Campos) to the nineteenth-century American bard. Ginsberg's access to Pessoa's poem comes through Edwin Honig and Susan M. Brown's translation entitled "Salutation to Walt Whitman."[8] He constructs his poem out of comparisons between himself and the Portuguese poet, but insists that he has not been influenced by reading Pessoa, having published *Howl* and other poems decades before encountering the Portuguese poet. And besides, even on this night ("Midnight April 12 88," following Pessoa's "June eleventh, nineteen hundred and fifteen"), Ginsberg admits to having read so far only a single page of Pessoa in translation. Let us take him at his word and quote only the first page of the Honig and Brown translation of "Salutation to Walt Whitman":

Infinite Portugal, June eleventh, nineteen hundred and fifteen . . .
A-hoy-hoy-hoy-hoy!

From here in Portugal, with all past ages in my brain,
I salute you, Walt, I salute you, my brother in the Universe,
I, with my monocle and tightly buttoned frock coat,
I am not unworthy of you, Walt, as you well know,
I am not unworthy of you, my greeting is enough to make it so . . .
I, so given to indolence, so easily bored,
I am with you, as you well know, and understand you and love you,
And though I never met you, born the same year you died,
I know you loved me too, you knew me, and I am happy.
I know that you knew me, that you considered and explained me,
I know that this is what I am, whether on Brooklyn Ferry ten years
    before I was born
Or strolling up Rua do Ouro thinking about everything that is not
    Rua do Ouro,
And just as you felt everything, so I feel everything, and so here we
    are clasping hands,
Clasping hands, Walt, clasping hands, with the universe doing a
    dance in our soul.

O singer of concrete absolutes, always modern and eternal,
Fiery concubine of the scattered world,
Great pederast brushing up against the diversity of things,
Sexualized by rocks, by trees, by people, by their trades,
Itch for the swiftly passing, for casual encounters, for what's merely
    observed,
My enthusiast for what's inside everything,
My great hero going straight through Death by leaps and bounds,
Roaring, screaming, bellowing greetings to God!

Singer of wild and gentle brotherhood with everything,
Great epidermic democrat, up close to it all in body and soul,
Carnival of each and every action, bacchanalia of all intentions,
Twin brother of every sudden impulse,
Jean-Jacques Rousseau of the world hell-bent to produce machinery,
Homer of all the *insaisissable* of wavering carnality,
Shakespeare of the sensation on the verge of steam propulsion,
Milton-Shelley of the dawning future of Electricity!
Incubus of all gestures,
Spasm penetrating every object-force,
Souteneur of the whole Universe,
Whore of all solar systems . . .[9]

I have quoted a bit more than the first page, choosing to end at a
natural break (assuming, as one might, that Ginsberg reading
the poem would have done the same), though further on he
could have read Campos's own admission, a justification for his
own decision to stop reading: "I can never read through all your
poems. . . . There's too much feeling in them."[10] Ginsberg's
"Salutations to Fernando Pessoa" reads:

Everytime I read Pessoa I think
I'm better than he is I do the same thing
more extravagantly—he's only from Portugal,
I'm American greatest Country in the world
right now End of XX Century tho Portugal
had a big empire in the 15th century never mind
now shrunk to a Corner of Iberian peninsula
whereas New York take New York for instance
tho Mexico City's bigger N.Y.'s richer think of Empire State
Building not long ago world empire's biggest skyscraper—

be that as't may I've experience 61 years' XX Century
Pessoa walked down Rua do Ouro only till 1936
He entered Whitman so I enter Pessoa no
matter what they say besides dead he wouldn't object.

What way'm I better than Pessoa?
Known on 4 Continents I have 25 English books he only 3
his mostly Portuguese, but that's not his fault—
U.S.A.'s a bigger Country
merely 2 Trillion in debt a passing freakout,
Reagan's dirty work an American Century aberration
unrepresenting our Nation Whitman sang in Epic manner
tho worried about in *Democratic Vistas*
As a Buddhist not proud my superiority to Pessoa
I'm humble Pessoa was nuts a big difference,
tho apparently gay—same as Socrates,
consider Michelangelo da Vinci Shakespeare
inestimable comrado Walt
True I was tainted Pinko at an early age a mere trifle
science itself destroys ozone layers this era antiStalinists
poison entire earth with radioactive anticommunism
Maybe I lied somewhat
rarely in verse, only protecting others' reputations.
Frankly too Candid about my mother tho meant well
Did Pessoa mention his mother? she's interesting,
powerful to birth sextuplets
Alberto Cairo [*sic*] Álvaro de Campos Ricardo Reis Bernardo Soares &
   Alexander Search simultaneously
with Fernando Pessoa himself a classic sexophrenic
Confusing personae not so popular
outside Portugal's tiny kingdom (till recently a second-rate police
   state)
Let me get to the point er I forget what it was
but certainly enjoy making comparisons between this Ginsberg &
   Pessoa
people talk about in Iberia hardly any books in English
presently the world's major diplomatic language extended throughout
   China.
Besides he was a shrimp, himself admits in interminable "Salutations to
   Walt Whitman"
whereas 5' 7¹/₂" height
somewhat above world average, no immodesty,
I'm speaking seriously about me & Pessoa.

Anyway he never influenced me, never read Pessoa
before I wrote my celebrated *Howl* already translated into
   24 languages,
not to this day's Pessoa influence an anxiety
Midnight April 12 '88 merely glancing his book
certainly influences me in passing, only reasonable
but reading a page in translation hardly proves "Influence."
Turning to Pessoa, what'd he write about? Whitman
(Lisbon, the sea etc.) method peculiarly longwinded,
diarrhea mouth some people say—Pessoa Schmessoa.
                    April 12, 1988[11]

The comparisons that Ginsberg makes are not just between
Pessoa the poet and Ginsberg the poet (themes and tech-
niques) but between Ginsberg the man and Pessoa the man
(sexual proclivities and physical stature) as well as between
languages (Portuguese and English) and countries (imperial
America and postimperial Portugal)—and these comparisons
are always to the Portuguese poet's disadvantage. Campos had
paid homage to Walt Whitman (his poem was a "salute" as well
as a "salutation"), but Ginsberg has no intention of directly
saluting Pessoa (he gives him his "salutations," whereas Honig
and Brown, in titling their translation of Campos's poem, had
retained Campos's singular form "Salutation"). Ginsberg
wishes to cut Pessoa down to size by seeing him for the
"shrimp" Pessoa admits to being when compared to himself:
Ginsberg measures "5' 7¹/₂''," which, he notes, is "somewhat
above world average."

But this measurement should give us pause. Pessoa might
admit being a shrimp, but his heteronym Álvaro de Campos is
"tall (1.75 meters tall, two centimeters more than I)," writes
Pessoa.[12] There is something silly, of course, about this measurement, but maybe that's the point. Take a look at some of the
other measurements. There is always something deflating in the
way Ginsberg presents them. America has New York (which is
the Empire State "tho Mexico City's bigger"), and New York has
the Empire State Building (which "not long ago world empire's
biggest skyscraper" but no longer so). Ginsberg has "25 English
books," Pessoa "only 3" (but Pessoa has any number of books in
Portuguese, not to mention translations in many languages,
and more coming over sixty years after his death in 1935 [not

1936, as Ginsberg has it]). Ginsberg, "being Buddhist," is "not proud of superiority to Pessoa," but Pessoa (in the guise of his heteronym Alberto Caeiro [not Cairo, as Ginsberg has it]) was introduced by Thomas Merton in the 1960s to American readers as something of a "Zen" poet.[13] Ginsberg calls Portugal a "tiny kingdom (till recently a second-rate police state)" but describes the U.S.A. as the "bigger Country / Merely 2 Trillion in debt"—"Reagan's dirty work." He describes this "Pessoa Schmessoa['s] . . . method peculiarly longwinded, diarrhea mouth some people say," but it is Ginsberg himself who wrote "Howl" and other "longwinded, diarrhea mouth" poems, as others might argue. And if Pessoa's themes are "Whitman, (Lisbon, the sea etc.)," what are Ginsberg's but New York, Whitman, etc.? In short, in this litany of comparisons we have Ginsberg sending himself up no less than Pessoa (and to a much lesser extent Whitman). We should not be surprised at this. After all, it was Ginsberg who added to "Howl" the comic, antitypical poem "A Supermarket in California," in which the speaker taunts: "I saw you, Walt Whitman, childless, lonely old grubber, poking among the meats in the refrigerator and eyeing the grocery boys. / I heard you asking questions of each: Who killed the pork chops? What price bananas? Are you my Angel?"[14] Ginsberg could not in 1955, when he wrote "A Supermarket in California," have been influenced by Campos's "Salutation to Walt Whitman" (though he did know García Lorca's "Oda a Walt Whitman"),[15] but if by some chance he had known the poem, he would have not have missed the playfulness of Álvaro de Campos's lines: "O singer of concrete absolutes, always modern and eternal, / Fiery concubine of the scattered world, / Great pederast brushing up against the diversity of things, / Sexualized by rocks, by trees, by people, by their trades, / Itch for the swiftly passing, for casual encounters, for what's merely observed."[16] Ginsberg's play in "Salutations to Fernando Pessoa" is cruder, his jokes broader, but by design they are not much different from Campos's jokingly serious play in "Salutation to Walt Whitman."

Still, what really bothers Ginsberg about Pessoa's audacious transoceanic, transcentury alliance with Whitman is simply that the Portuguese poet claimed it first. Writing in 1915, he anticipated Ginsberg's first published acknowledgments of

Whitman by a full four decades. In the mid-1950s Ginsberg mentions Whitman briefly in "Siesta in Xbalba" and composes a rather straightforward (for Ginsberg) "Love Poem on Theme by Whitman," but there is no Whitman poem by Ginsberg to rival Campos's "Saudação a Walt Whitman" in playful audacity until "A Supermarket in California" (1955). And there is nothing in Ginsberg to rival Campos's wholehearted commitment to Walt until his 1984 poem "I Love Old Whitman So," published in *White Shroud: Poems, 1980-1985*. Since he did not have the first exuberant word in the matter, let Ginsberg have the next to last subdued word here:

Youthful, caressing, boisterous, tender
Middle aged thoughtful, ten thousand noticings of shore ship or street,
workbench, forest, household or office, opera—
that conning his paper book again to read aloud to those few Chinese
    boys & girls
who know enough American tongue to ear his hand—
loath to select one leaf from another, loath to reject a sympathetic page
—the tavern boy's look, a stone prisoner's mustache-sweat, prostitute in
    the sun, garrulous old man waving goodbye on the stoop—
I skim *Leaves* beginning to end, this year in the Middle Kingdom
marvel his swimmers huffing naked on the wave
and touched by his desperado farewell, "Who touches this book touches
    a man"
tip the hat on my skull
to the old soldier, old sailor, old writer, old homosexual, old Christ poet
    journeyman,
inspired in middle age to chaunt Eternity in Manhattan,
and see the speckled snake & swelling orb earth vanish
after green seasons Civil War and years of snow
white hair.[17]

Ginsberg continued to admire Whitman, we know, and he continued to assign Pessoa to his students.

7

Blue Tiles

Joyce Carol Oates

By the mid-1990s Joyce Carol Oates, novelist, poet, playwright, and essayist, had published more than twenty collections of short stories. Buried in that rich hoard is *"The Poisoned Kiss" and Other Stories from the Portuguese.* Her eighth story collection, it "remains an anomaly in Oates's oeuvre," writes one critic, "an experiment in fiction (and in consciousness) that . . . provides a fascinating gloss on her ongoing exploration of psychological states."[1] Attributed to one "Fernandes de Briao," this book of stories that came to Oates through "either real or imagined 'possession'" presents the student of Pessoa's influence on English-language poets with a singular opportunity.[2] It is possible to link this 1975 book suggestively with Fernando Pessoa, who was also "possessed" by his heteronyms, and to several Pessoan or near-Pessoan texts. In "Fernandes" Oates has devised her own Portuguese heteronym, one that, like Pessoa's major heteronyms, has also produced a body of work that can be read, interpreted, judged. Yet nowhere has Oates acknowledged having read Pessoa when she wrote her "Portuguese" stories or even having heard of him.

The Poisoned Kiss is comprised of twenty-two stories, an opening note, and an afterword. The book has a portmanteau authorship according to the title page—Fernandes/Joyce Carol Oates. Many, if not all, of its stories appeared originally in magazines, such as *Carolina Quarterly, Chelsea, December, Harper's Bazaar, Literary Review, Massachusetts Review, Partisan Review, Prism International, Southwest Review, Transatlantic Review, Aspen Leaves, Yale Review,* and *Sparrow.* In the journals and magazines, authorship of these stories was usually handled clearly but misleadingly. When "The Letter" appeared in the *Literary Review* (1973) there were author's notes for both Oates and Fernandes de Briao, while the story itself was identified as the word of Fernandes in a translation "from the Portuguese by Joyce Carol Oates."[3] Similarly, when "Letters to Fernandes from a Young American Poet" appeared in *Chelsea* (1972), the contents page identified its author as "Fernandes (de Briao)" and, at the end of the story, Joyce Carol Oates as its translator.[4] Both "Fernandes" and Oates merited identification in the notes on contributors. Interestingly, Oates was credited with a recent novel, *Wonderland*, as well as a play, "The Ontological Proof of My Existence." Nothing was said about her translations from the Portuguese. "Fernandes," on the other hand, is described: "Fernandes (de Briao) lives in Lisbon, was educated partly at Harvard, is in his fifties and does translations. His stories have not been printed in Portugal but have appeared here in the *Literary Review, Massachusetts Review*. This story is from a group called *Azulejos*, most of which are unpublished."[5] Credits for "Two Young Men," which appeared as the lead story in the second number of *Aspen Leaves* in 1974, are handled differently. On the contents page it is listed as "a story by Joyce Carol Oates"; but within the magazine the story is identified as a translation "from the Portuguese of Fernandes."[6] There is a contributor's note for Oates but none, this time, for "Fernandes." When "Loss" appeared in the *Southwest Review* (1971), it was noted that Fernandes de Briao is "itself a pen name" of a writer who holds "a degree from Harvard" and is now "retired." "Like his present translator, he does translations as well as original stories."[7] When "Parricide" appeared in the *Yale Review* (1974), while it was indicated that the story was "translated from the Portuguese of Fernandes de Briao," all possible ambiguity disappeared in the note on Oates, which reads "Joyce Carol Oates is a novelist and short-story writer. A collection of short stories, of which 'Parricide' is one, will be published under the title *The Poisoned Kiss*."[8]

The Poisoned Kiss employs a five-line epigraph from the poetry of Saint John of the Cross. It is given in the original Spanish:

Oh noche, que guiaste,
Oh noche amable más que el alborada:
Oh noche, que juntaste
Amado con amada,
Amada en el Amado transformada!

Its English translation, by the South African poet Roy Campbell, is relegated to a note at the bottom of the page:

Oh night that was my guide!
Oh darkness dearer than the morning's pride,
Oh night that joined the lover
To the beloved bride
Transfiguring them each into the other!

Oates's epigraphic use of lines from Campbell's translation introduces the notion that her stories carry some curious overall Iberian baggage.

The stories by "Fernandes" came inexplicably to Oates out of the blue. Not only had she not visited Portugal, but the country held no interest for her. Admittedly, she later looked up friends who provided her with some firsthand knowledge of Portuguese details, but she did not seek such information until Fernandes's "possession" of her had all but exhausted itself. "The Fernandes stories came out of nowhere," she wrote in a note dated March 1975, continuing:

If I did not concentrate deliberately on my own work, or if I allowed myself to daydream or become overly exhausted, my mind would move—it would seem to swerve or leap—into "Portugal." There seemed to be a great pressure, a series of visions, that demanded a formal, aesthetic form; I was besieged by Fernandes—story after story, some no more than sketches or paragraphs that tended to crowd out my own writing. I was able to alternate a "Fernandes" story with one of my own or with a chapter from the novel I was writing (*Wonderland*), as a kind of bargain; otherwise, Fernandes would have overwhelmed me. [188]

Since Oates published *Wonderland* in 1971, it seems likely that the original versions of the "Fernandes" stories were written between late 1970 and 1971. Later, when asked to explain how *The Poisoned Kiss* had come into being, with its fictional character as a "collaborator" who gives the book "a sort of visionary glow," she answered:

> The appeal of writing—of any kind of *artistic* activity—is primarily the investigation of mystery. Somehow, by employing a deliberate speech-rhythm, or by unlocking it, one is able to follow a course into the psyche that reveals different facets of the self. *The Poisoned Kiss* is my journal of a sort of the most extreme experience of my own along these lines: Actually, I gave to the *voice* of the stories the adjective "Portuguese" because I knew only that it was foreign, yet not familiarly foreign. Beyond this, it is difficult to speak.
>
> I should stress, though, that the *voice* of these tales was firmly joined to a fairly naturalistic setting by way of subsequent research and conversations with friends who knew Portugal well. And the tales were rigorously written and rewritten.[9]

Revealed in this seemingly straightforward explanation is the claim that there was nothing intrinsically Portuguese about the voice of the narrator who intruded himself and his narratives on the author's consciousness. Oates knew the voice was "foreign, yet not familiarly foreign," and therefore she chose to call it "Portuguese" and to give that voice the Portuguese surname of "Fernandes." In a 1987 essay surveying the subject of writers who have chosen to employ pseudonyms and who sometimes create pseudonymous selves, Oates concludes: "In the end, it is probable that the cultivation of a pseudonym is not so very different from the cultivation *in vivo* of the narrative voice that sustains any work of words, making it unique and inimitable. Choosing a pseudonym as the work's formal author simply takes the mysterious process a step or two further, erasing the author's social identity and supplanting it with the pseudonymous identity."[10] Interestingly, this statement closes out not only the essay but the entire collection, even as the penultimate sentence of her "Preface" reads: "My essay on 'pseudonymous selves' . . . is probably as personal a document, in the interstices of its elaboration of others' obsessions, as anything I have ever written."[11]

Thus Oates discovered a pseudonym for the stories that were coming to her, almost willy-nilly, in a "foreign" voice, called it "Portuguese," and assigned that fictitious voice a Portuguese name. But she did not remove herself from the book's title page, since she presents herself as something of a coauthor —Fernandes/Joyce Carol Oates, and she signs the Afterword with her own name alone. Yet in an unsigned prefatory "Note," she fudges the coauthorship suggested by the title page by insisting on her role as the *fictitious* Fernandes's translator: "The tales in this collection are translated from an imaginary work, *Azulejos,* by an imaginary author, Fernandes de Briao. To the best of my knowledge he has no existence and has never existed, though without his very real guidance I would not have had access to the mystical 'Portugal' of the stories—nor would I have been compelled to recognize the authority of a world-view quite antithetical to my own" (15). Notice here the nice touch in choosing to entitle Fernandes's book *Azulejos (Blue Tiles),* which not only refers to those quintessentially Portuguese artifacts dating back some five centuries but also evokes the title of the weekly to which the young Mário de Sá-Carneiro, Pessoa's close friend and fellow poet, contributed his first stories and poems.[12] But notice too that Briao, Fernandes's unlikely last name, would seem to call for a tilde over the *a.*

Here, then, is a pseudonymous work, whose pseudonymity is undermined by its being called a translation of an "imaginary" work and by the author's revealing herself first as something of its coauthor, then its translator, and finally its author.

Fernando Pessoa and his heteronyms go unnamed in *The Poisoned Kiss* and in Oates's essay "Pseudonymous Selves." But it is not surprising that they do, for, remarkably, Jorge Luis Borges's name is also absent from both texts. And yet no reader of *The Poisoned Kiss* who knows Pessoa's poetry and his "nonexistent coterie" of heteronymic selves can escape the feeling that there is a strong connection between Pessoa's work and Oates's. For Pessoa anticipates closely—in example, theme, and even, at times, detail—this "Fernandes/Oates." Do not the stories in *The Poisoned Kiss,* particularly those that express a form of no-nonsense philosophical naturalism, echo Pessoa? This, of course, is the great theme of the poems by the pagan Alberto Caeiro, who is master to Pessoa's other major poetic heteronyms—Álvaro de Campos and Ricardo Reis—and to Fernando Pessoa himself, even if we do not consider "Fernando

Pessoa" to be, as the Portuguese poet-critic Jorge de Sena did, a fourth major poetic heteronym. In "Fernandes" Oates has constructed her version of a typical Pessoan mind, a labyrinth that outriddles Borges, even as Pessoa's does.[13] "Fernandes" is a heteronymic gray eminence with his own American follower.

In "Letters to Fernandes from a Young American Poet," Oates has Fernandes imagine an epistolary story in which an acolyte, with whom he shares a love-hate relationship, urges him to read Walt Whitman. "Up most of the night drinking and reading," he writes: "Read Whitman: 'Agonies are one of my changes of garments.' And: 'Unscrew the locks from the doors! Unscrew the doors from their jambs!' Do you know what he means?" (139). The young American is also responsible for a translation of *The Sheathed Son of God,* a work by Fernandes's friend António, who is now hidden away in one of the prisons or hospitals maintained by the Portuguese dictator António Salazar. The poet António must be freed; the messages of his *Legends* must not die.

António's anarchy and love, António's simplicity . . . Can't explain. Can't explain why we must come to grips with António's vision, why cross & recross that Dark River of his when it is so painful. Bringing the much-folded, much-unfolded, much-folded petition to Pedra de Myra, too old, blind. Bringing it around to the five or six young poets you introduced me to—their bold signatures—"bold"—as if they know they will not be blamed. They are of good families, like you.

. . . trying to understand you and your people, Fernandes. You are all sleepwalkers. Can you explain yourself to me?

All A's books, all the *Legends,* are banned here. You have lived with this for years. Will you never do anything about it? When the language is erased we will all be erased. Pray, sink your fingers into your eyes, you beloved of Our Lady of Stone and of Dr. S[alazar], who has done 'so much a foreigner can't understand . . . ' We will all be erased, all of us. [141]

Later, foreshadowing Allen Ginsberg's competition with the Whitman-like Álvaro de Campos, Fernandes's young American poet boasts both that he is "six foot three, Fernandes, taller even than you!" and that he has worked his "way through the North American consciousness-slop" in which so many young poets are "permanently stuck" (143). "A" has a message, like that of the poet of *Mensagem*, who calls for an empire of the Spirit.

A must be freed, will be freed, if I have to die over here. If A and I both have to die. I have talked for hours, for days, w/people here who should understand, tried to project my idea (basically A's) of how the country could be transformed, nothing blown up or thrown into the air & raining down but a Spiritual change so much more violent—how all the countries of the world could be transformed, even the United States—what A saw, what he tried to make us see in his *Legends*.
. . . Must push ourselves out to the very edge of the Spirit.
. . . Must learn what A means by being 'the beginning people.' [145]

Oates's story is set somewhat later than the 1930s, the decade in which Pessoa died. It is not surprising, therefore, that the narrative reflects subsequent Portuguese history and attacks Salazar's fascist policies as they played out in succeeding decades. Oates's young American poet begins with a warning to Fernandes and then turns to a characterization of Portugal in the early 1970s:

I know you have left Lisbon. Don't dare to leave the country because that would look bad, but you've left Lisbon & are hiding somewhere. You have your own chapels, eh? And your own private priests? Is that how you people worship, on your humble obedient knees in front of the Virgin & her dreamy deathliness? But I could love her, yes—even her!—if A loved her—I could embrace her in all her stone, even her, even you!—if A showed me the way. Hatred for the Catholic-fascist-racist-colonizing-Martianizing culture—that was A's curse—but love for the faces, the beautiful faces, the Suffering we must endure in our loneliness—that was his sweetest burden, a curse too, because he couldn't escape. [148]

It is interesting to note that Oates first published "Letters to Fernandes from a Young American Poet" in 1972, *before* the overthrow of the nearly fifty-year-old fascist regime in Portugal on April 25, 1974. Pessoa's own attitude toward Salazar's regime in its early years and its more moderate stages is summarized by Jacinto do Prado Coelho, one of his most perceptive readers: "In no way, in working out *Mensagem*, does the author identify with the official nationalism of 1934, catholic-apostolic, monolithic, rapacious and hypocritical, adorned with the fascist rhetoric of imperialist mystic lore."[14] Notably, Pessoa had begun to satirize the character and personality of the architect of the so-called New State in poems he wrote—but knew he could not publish—in the last summer of his life. Jorge de Sena discovered these poems among the poet's papers in 1954 and published them in 1960 in Brazil and Portugal.[15]

Not all the stories in *The Poisoned Kiss* are as suggestively linked to Pessoa as "Letters to Fernandes" seems to be. Yet I would call attention to two or three others that seem to be richly evocative of a Pessoan world. The Pessoa who wrote a trilogy of poems on the Saints—António, João, and Pedro—and the heteronymic Alberto Caeiro who wrote of the return of the baby Jesus to earth in poem 8 of *The Keeper of Sheep* would have found something familiar in Oates's opening story. "Our Lady of the Easy Death of Alferce" centers on a statue of the Virgin, which, to her great astonishment, after centuries of holding the baby Jesus with its visage away from her, is finally able to look upon its face when a fanatic breaks the child from her arms and drops him to the floor. Pessoa might also have admired the Pessoan lineaments of "Plagiarized Material," with its strong touches of Borges and of Kafka's "The Burrow." In this penultimate story of *The Poisoned Kiss*, the famous writer "Cabral" is pleased to write in fragments, much like Pessoa's semi-heteronym Bernardo Soares in his *Book of Disquiet*, and is in no hurry to put the pieces together into a single whole.

Cabral had received dozens of letters from magazine editors, begging him for contributions of any length; even paragraphs or parts of paragraphs. And so he had no reason to hurry, to rush his aesthetic theory into print. In fact, he rather liked the method forced upon him by the multiplicity of journals: he believed in fragments, essentially. He preferred fragments. Like those hideous blue and white *azulejos* found everywhere in the country, his work was basically in parts, not wholes, and must be put together by someone else, someone who believed in the trashy happiness of the *total picture*. [172]

Honored though he is, Cabral is skeptical of both what others take to be reality and the putative reality of words. But he will suffer his comeuppance. Fate will undo him in the person of

an unknown plagiarist, who not only successfully plagiarizes
Cabral's published work but who also uncannily anticipates his
as yet unwritten work, thus beating him into print. Cabral's final
recourse is one of desperation. He will return the favor, he will
play the plagiarist's own game by anticipating what the plagiarist will say of Cabral in an obituary. Yet his desperation continues, for he now fears that his plagiarist will surely alter his
obituary. End of story. Cabral's very existence has given body to
Oates's Pessoan aphorism: "The more deliberate the writer is in
his art, the more he risks by existing."[16]

8

Durban Echoes

Charles Eglington

The 1989 *Penguin Book of Southern African Verse*, compiled by Stephen Gray, includes poetry by Luís de Camões, Fernando Pessoa, and Joaquim Paço d'Arcos, three Portuguese nationals. The last named is not important to this consideration of Charles Eglington. The other two are.

The collection starts out with canto 5 of Camões's *Os Lusíadas* in Sir Richard Fanshawe's seventeenth-century translation. Fernando Pessoa, considered by Gray to be an essentially 1930s Camonean presence in southern African literature, is represented by five poems, three of them drawn from the "Mar português" section of *Mensagem*, a suite of elegiac poems celebrating with no inconsiderable irony the tragedy of Portugal's glorious past.[1]

The importance of canto 5 of *Os Lusíadas* to southern African literature lies in its introduction of the figure of Adamastor, the personified "Spirit of the Cape." It tells of the first Portuguese encounters with Africans and of their difficulties in trying to navigate the Cape of Storms. That Camões did not appear in the 1968 version of the *Penguin Book of South African Verse*, compiled by Jack Cope and Uys Krige, makes it even more pertinent to ask why Gray includes him in an anthology devoted to southern African poetry. "Historic" in its own right, argues Gray, canto 5 of *Os Lusíadas* stands at the very beginning of southern African literary history.[2]

Camões could not have imagined that Adamastor would come to function as such, but his symbolic figure soon came "to symbolize all the horrors and tribulations of Portuguese maritime history compressed into one."[3] As Gray writes, Adamastor, "the white man's creation myth of Africa," is "at the root of all the subsequent white semiology invented to cope with the African experience."[4] As the European sees it, "[Adamastor] belongs to an older but defeated culture, and is likely to sink the new European enlightenment if allowed within its purlieu; although his size is gigantic, his responses are essentially childish and they obey paternalistic directives; he is capable of love, but only carnally, so that if he advances too presumptuously he is to be humiliated and rendered impotent."[5] But he possesses "Titanic force," which is "not only the pent power of a vast and frighteningly unknown continent, populated by serpents and burning stones, but a symbol of the awe with which Africa was regarded in early experiences of the untamed."[6] But if "*The Lusiads* is the national epic of the Lusitanian bogeymen, the sons of its eponymous hero, Lusus," it is the critical task of Africans to reexamine *Os Lusíadas* "by a reverse-angle shot, as it were," for they must "look at Camoens from the vantage point of the cruel, dark and vengeful interior that he and his hero viewed as unfit for human habitation."[7] Gray then tracks the presence of Adamastor in several southern African works, including Roy Campbell's "Rounding the Cape" (1926):

The low sun whitens on the flying squalls,
Against the cliffs the long grey surge is rolled
Where Adamastor from his marble halls
Threatens the sons of Lusus as of old.

Faint on the glare uptowers the dauntless form,
Into whose shade abysmal as we draw,
Down on our decks, from far above the storm,
Grin the stark ridges of his broken jaw.

Across his back, unheeded, we have broken
Whole forests: heedless of the blood we've spilled,
In thunder still his prophecies are spoken,
In silence, by the centuries, fulfilled.

Farewell, terrific shade! though I go free
Still of the powers of darkness art thou Lord:
I watch the phantom sinking in the sea
Of all that I have hated or adored.

The prow glides smoothly on through seas quiescent:
But where the last point sinks into the deep,
The land lies dark beneath the rising crescent,
And Night, the Negro, murmurs in his sleep.[8]

Campbell wrote his poem aboard ship as he was leaving South Africa. "For the first time," writes his biographer, "Campbell can see South Africa whole."[9] He personifies the country as Camões's black giant Adamastor standing before a dark continent. Campbell's vantage point is that of one going off to voluntary exile, distancing himself from this Lord's "powers of darkness."

In this context it is useful to turn to Pessoa's "O Mostrengo," a poem published in *Mensagem*. Recognizing the appropriateness of including the poem as one of the southern African transformations of the Adamastor myth, Gray anthologizes it as the work of an "Afro-Portuguese" poet, in Charles Eglington's translation as "The Blighter (after Fernando Pessoa)."[10] The poem opens out the passage in Camões's *Os Lusíadas* in which the Portuguese sailors come up against the personified Spirit of the Cape. Like Campbell's "Rounding the Cape," "O Mostrengo" is also written from the "outside" of Africa, not from "under the horizon"—that is to say, from the African point of view:

The blighter that is at the end of the sea
On the pitch-black night raised itself flying;
Round the vessel it flew three times,
Three times it flew creaking,
And said, "Who dared pierce
Into my dens that I do not reveal,
My black ceilings of the end of the world?"
And the helmsman said, trembling,
"His Majesty King John the Second!"

"Whose sails are these then which I rub against?
Whose the keels I see and hear?"
Said the blighter, and rolled three times,
Three times it rolled filthy and bulky,
"Who attempts what is solely my power,
I who abide where no one ever could see me
And who drip the fears of the depthless sea?"
And the helmsman trembled, and said,
"His Majesty King John the Second!"

Three times he raised his hands from the helm,
Three times he had them rooted on the helm,
And said after trembling three times,
"Here at the helm I am more than myself:
I am a People who wants the sea that is yours;
And more than the blighter, that my soul fears
And rolls on the darkness of the end of the world,
Orders the will, that ties me at the helm,
Of His Majesty King John the Second!" [9]

Jack Cope, who edited *Under the Horizon*, the posthumous collection of Eglington's poetry, says of "The Blighter" that it was the "nearest" Eglington "got to a straight translation" of Pessoa (xii). Eglington was nearly forty when he discovered Pessoa, but Pessoa's "appeal" was immediate and, as he wrote, "immense" (95). He tried to translate other poems by Pessoa but could not carry them through. Invariably, each one turned into an original poem. "Pessoa has a curious effect on me," he confessed, "I begin to translate one of his poems, and before I know where I am I have abandoned the translation and begun a poem of my own. In the finished result the prima anima of my own poem derives from the theme, some of the images or the main idea, of Pessoa's poems" (xi).[11]

Several of the poems in which Pessoa's poems are the prima anima were published in Eglington's lifetime. In *Contrast 16*, (1967), Eglington published "Homage to Fernando Pessoa," a selection of his "Pessoan" poems. Of the four poems chosen, three (numbered one to three) seem to constitute a suite of poems, while the fourth and last poem goes unnumbered. The block of four poems is preceded by an epigraph consisting of three lines from "Horizonte," a poem in *Mensagem:* "Buscar na linha fria do horizonte / A árvore, a praia, a flor, a ave, a fonte— / Os beijos merecidos da Verdade"—which Eglington renders as "To seek the cold line of the horizon / Tree, beach, flower, bird and fountain— / The deserved kisses of Truth" (16).[12] He also uses a two-line epigraph in "Lourenço Marques," the fourth and last poem: "Ó mar salgado, quanto do teu sal / São lagrimas de Portugal!" ("Oh salty sea how much of your salt / Is the tears of Portugal!"[13] Like "Lourenço Marques," the first three poems also stem from *Mensagem.*

In *Under the Horizon* these poems are presented differently. There are no longer any epigraphs as such. The epigraphic lines from "Horizonte" that in the journal publication were assigned to all four poems and the epigraphic lines assigned specifically to "Lourenço Marques," along with additional lines from Pessoa's "Epitáfio de Bartolomeu Dias," are now quoted between poems in such a way that they cannot be interpreted single-mindedly as epigraphs to specific poems. Ingeniously, the epigraphs are deployed over this suite of four poems, incorporated to serve as lead-ins to the poems they seem to be closest to. As such, they do double duty, introducing individual poems while standing out as unobtrusive blocks in the suite's overall echo structure. "Horizon" is still preceded by the lines from "Horizonte"; "Bartholomew Diaz" is now preceded by lines from "Epitáfio de Bartolomeu Dias"—"Jaz aqui, na pequena praia extrema, / O Capitão do Fim" ("Here lies on the ultimate small beach / The Final Captain";[14] "Fever" is now preceded by lines from "Padrão"—"E faz a febre em mim navegar / Só encontrará em Deus" ("And makes the fever in me explore / Only to encounter through God")[15]; and "Lourenço Marques" is preceded by the same lines from "Mar português."

Just how Eglington turned the Pessoan *prima anima* into these original poems can be suggested by looking at "Bartholomew Diaz," the second poem in the "Homage to Fernando Pessoa" suite. This poem breaks into five quatrains. The opening quatrain is a translation of the four lines of Pessoa's poem "Epitáfio de Bartolomeu Dias":

> At last he reached the ultimate small beach,
> The final captain. Wonderment is furled—
> The sea remains the same—none fears it now!
> High on his shoulder Atlas holds the world. [4]

Eglington then goes on to build his poem out of this translation, not by going outside Pessoa's *Mensagem,* but by drawing into his expansion of Pessoa, lines, images, and terms from other poems in *Mensagem.* His second quatrain reads:

> He who had ventured past Cape Bojador
> To raid the fortress of abyss and storm,

Saw overhead the minatory stars
And at his prow the ignis fatuus form. [4]

These lines build freely on borrowings from "Mar português"
that are close enough to encourage one to see Eglington's lines
as ironic commentary on the original (consider that his Bartolomeu Dias is on a "raid"):

He who will sail beyond Cape Bojador
Has to push beyond pain.
God gave the sea its abyss, its dangers,
But in the sea He mirrored the heavens.[16]

Eglington's third quatrain continues the dialogue with Pessoa,
appropriating imagery from still another poem from *Mensagem*. Here is Eglington:

Horizons that deceived with sensitive
Configurations, till at last a tower
Rose on the sky, a bird cried out and land
Burst through a mist of longing into flower. [4]

Here is the middle stanza of Pessoa's "Horizonte":

That far-off rigid coastline—
When the ship approaches, the shore now rises
With the trees, where the distance offered nothing;
Closer, land breaks into sounds and colors;
As we disembark, come birds and flowers,
Where before was but a far-off abstract line.[17]

The fourth quatrain returns us to the overall situation presented by Pessoa in "Mar português," but with a difference. It
takes up Bartolomew Dias's experience as he returns home,
having to round Bojador once again but this time in the opposite direction. It reads:

And when, returning, he sailed past the cape
Whose saurian menace he had met and spurned,
The Tagus flowed to meet him in a light
That from the once-dark headland brightly burned. [4]

Eglington then concludes his poem:

> Now distances have fountains, trees and birds;
> Each cold horizon is the silver beach
> That shelters him—for which he dared the seas
> And sailed past all extremities to reach. [4]

This stanza plays off against the final lines, not of "Epitáfio de Bartolomeu Dias," but of "Horizonte":

> To dream is to see from some vague distance
> Shapes invisible, then with the quickened
> Motion of one's hope and will,
> To seek upon the cold horizon
> Tree and beach, flower, bird, and fountain—
> Those kisses Truth awards.[18]

Fully in keeping with Eglington's sense of what happened to him when he tried to translate Pessoa is the fact that, when he did write the poem he entitled "Horizon," he drew nothing from Pessoa's "Horizonte" beyond the inspiration accorded him by the title and by the poem's definition of "horizon" as "the low horizon's thin, cold line." Eglington's "Horizon," expanding and stretching Pessoa's phrase, reads:

> The early mariners perhaps
> Were first to understand the pure
> Aesthetic of horizons: chart
> And instrument were insecure
> Against the treacheries of sky
> And ocean; often as they watched
> They saw the ancient portents fade
> On winds of promise, or reveal
> Their shining menace; then, afraid
> Because they found no hallowed sign
> To prosper them, they sought in awe
> The low horizon's thin, cold line. [3][19]

Somewhat different is Eglington's strategy in "Fever," which takes off from imagery in Pessoa's "Padrão." While Pessoa's poem is a testamentary monologue in the voice of the navigator Diogo Cão, Eglington's poem is spoken by an unnamed narrator who addresses Pessoa as "Fernando," compares himself (and others) to Diogo Cão, talks about tides that are not oceanic but "stellar," and substitutes for an "earthly port" an "astral terminal." Pessoa's (and Camões's) argonauts have given way, in 1967, to astronauts. *Mensagem*'s Diogo Cão has a "fever" for navigation that will find its eternally calm, earthly port through God, but Eglington's navigator has a "fever" that "seeks its balm / In knowledge that can still / The fear of unknown things" (5). The last poem in the "Homage to Fernando Pessoa" suite is "Lourenço Marques." Twice it refers to the "backward-looking" Pessoa's sadness, focusing on this Portuguese-created "city, grown and prosperous," that now shows only "the future's brooding innocence."

> Its world, though growing old, is young.
> Its rooted heritage is germinal:
> Behind its tall, proud back a continent
> Throws out a challenge, like the oceans once. [7]

This is the kind of poem that Fernando Pessoa might have written about the fading Portuguese presence in Lourenço Marques's African future (that is to say, a future that might exclude the Portuguese themselves), had he had the benefit, say, of not being himself Portuguese.

Eglington has left a clear statement of what he was attempting to do in "Homage to Fernando Pessoa." In a note accompanying the publication of the four poems in *Contrast 16* in 1967, Eglington writes:

Pessoa used the heteronyms [Alberto Caeiro, Ricardo Reis, and Álvaro de Campos] to express different aspects of his complex personality—and the differences are astonishing. In my *Homage* I am concerned only with "Fernando Pessoa," and especially with the poems he wrote between 1918 and 1934 which are contained in *Mensagem* (Message). They deal with the Portuguese past, with the age of the great princes and captains, with the great mariners and discoverers. He dwells also—in a subtle and sublime mood of hope—on the decline of that age. These poems represent the backward-looking Pessoa—who could miraculously co-exist with the forward-looking, futuristic, avant-garde Álvaro de Campos. They are among the purest, the most mysterious and magical, of his lyrics.

My poems are not translations, nor are they "after Pessoa." But their *prima anima* is to be found in the *Mensagem* poems, and more particularly in a number of phrases, images and concepts which are central to them. [98-99]

Jennings argues that, in identifying *Mensagem* as a "backward-looking" work, Eglington misreads "the intention of *Mensagem* as a whole." Jennings's Pessoa is "no less forward-looking" than the (quoting Eglington) "forward-looking, futuristic, avant-garde Álvaro de Campos," for, like T.S. Eliot, "Pessoa 'gathers the voices of the past and projects them into the future' and the message is, in brief, what had been done in the past can be done on a higher level in the future."[20]

Jennings's reading of *Mensagem* is consensual. But there are those readers who would disagree, preferring to find in *Mensagem* the nostalgic irony that Eglington indicates. Indeed, it might well be that Eglington's reading is closer to the reading that Pessoa's own ironic mind might give *Mensagem* than any reading that takes the poem as plainly predictive of a future Empire of the Portuguese Spirit. For, cannot this collection of poems itself be read as an exemplary *saudosista* poem? Did the poet not intend to evoke the symbols of a national obsession with defining and displaying the characteristics of the Portuguese spirit, that "longing, yearning, of sad personal recollection in the sun"—a bittersweet malaise that enables one to extend one's nostalgia even to the future?[21]

In *Under the Horizon* first place is given over to "Homage to Fernando Pessoa" as the opening poem in "Compass," the first section of the book. Eglington had planned it that way, asserts Jack Cope, for Pessoa was one of the two major forces in Eglington's work, the other being the British war poet Wilfred Owen. To Eglington, as it turned out, both poets were dangerous stars to steer by. Eglington's suicide, at the age of fifty-two, has been "explained" in terms of his obsessions with Pessoa and Owen. In his last weeks, "when his wife pleaded with him to say what was on his mind," reveals Cope, his only reply was "It is my demon" (xx). Cope, who had noticed well before Eglington's death that the author of "Homage" was "steeped in the Pessoa legend,"[22] speculates that Eglington "had tried to work through what Pessoa called a 'frustrated sexual inversion'" (xx). "Late in life he became increasingly conscious," continues Cope, "that the balance between the masculine and feminine polarities which seems to be markedly present in the 'divided selves' of most creative artists was coming down on the feminine side, amounting to a compulsive drive towards homosexuality." "Complexities of a like kind" had been met by both Owen and Pessoa "in their own ways" (xviii). To help explain Eglington's situation as man and artist, as well as locate the source of the pressures that finally caused him to take his life, Cope quotes Jennings's translation of a passage from one of Pessoa's unpublished prefaces:

I do not have any difficulty in defining myself. I have a feminine temperament with a masculine intelligence. My sensibility and the movements that come from it, and in which the temperament and its expression consist, are those of a woman. My faculties of relation, the intelligence and the will, which is the intelligence of impulse—are those of a man.

As to sensibility, when I say that I always like to be loved and never to love, I have said all. It always irks me to be obliged by the duty of common reciprocity—a certain loyalty of spirit—to respond. I enjoy passivity. I like only to give enough of activity to stimulate, so that I am not forgotten, the activity in loving of the one who would love me.

I recognise without illusion the nature of the phenomenon. It is a frustrated sexual inversion. It remains in the spirit. Always, however, in moments of meditation on myself, it disquiets me. I have never had the certainty, and I do not have it yet, that this disposition of temperament would not one day descend to the body. I do not say that I would practise the sexuality correspondent to that impulse; but even the desire would be enough to humiliate me. Several of us are of that kind—above all in artistic history. Shakespeare and Rousseau are the most illustrious examples. And my fear of that inversion of spirit descending into my body is rooted in the contemplation of how it descended in those two—completely and into pederasty in the first; uncertainly, in a vague masochism, in the second. [xviii-xix][23]

Cope also calls attention to the fact that one of Pessoa's major heteronyms—Álvaro de Campos ("probably the most important after Fernando Pessoa")—was, in Cope's word, "a homosexual" (xix).

All this speculation, suggestive though it may be, is not, at the last, definitive. After all, it is Pessoa's public poetry—in *Mensagem*—that Eglington turns to in "Homage to Fernando

Pessoa," not the poetry of Pessoa's most extroverted heteronym, Álvaro de Campos (who seems, more exactly, to be a
bisexual). Eglington's interest lay mainly with the grand historical myth that Pessoa constructed to his own complex ends, not
with the free-thinking Álvaro de Campos, an avatar of his own
shadowy self.[24]

9

Looking for Mr. Person

Michael Hamburger, John Wain, Andrew Harvey, and Dennis Silk

In his essays on Pessoa in the American periodicals *Poetry* (1955) and the *Literary Review* (1963), Edouard Roditi did some of the early critical spadework necessary to introduce Pessoa both as a reputable English-language poet and as a universal poet in any language. He also collaborated with Paul Celan, it will be recalled, to introduce Pessoa to a German audience, an effort that might have had the unexpected, belated effect of reintroducing Pessoa to the English in the late 1960s. For Celan's earliest English translator, the German-born English writer Michael Hamburger, could well have seen the Celan-Roditi translations of Pessoa in *Die Neue Rundschau* in 1956, three or four years after Hamburger and Celan had met in London on one of Celan's "rare" visits from Paris.[1] Hamburger's pages on Pessoa in *The Truth of Poetry: Tensions in Modern Poetry from Baudelaire to the 1960s,* first published in 1969 and reissued in 1982 and 1997, constitute one of the best critical interpretations of Pessoa in English. Describing the author of *Men-sagem* as "the most extreme case of multiple personality and self-division in modern poetry," Hamburger focuses his discussion around Pessoa's three major heteronyms—Reis, Caeiro, and Campos.[2] Managing in the course of a half dozen pages to suggest important ways in which Pessoa's poetry can profitably be compared with the work of Gottfried Benn, Hart Crane, and T.S. Eliot, he concludes with a shrewd attempt at explaining how Pessoa's various disguises relate to his underlying truthfulness: "It is the feelings of the empirical self which poetry enlarges, complements or even replaces with fictitious ones, but only because the empirical self is not the whole self, cramped as it is in its shell of convention, habit and circumstance. Pessoa's disguises did not impair his truthfulness because he used them not to hoodwink others, but to explore reality and establish the full identity of his multiple, potential selves."[3] Needing illustrative translations of Pessoa's poetry that he could not find, Hamburger translated "the things" for himself.[4]

Pessoa comes up in an early 1980s review by Hamburger of a book on Rilke. "Rilke's poetic personae were hardly less various than those of Fernando Pessoa," he writes, "though he did not resort to heteronyms except in a single instance, and his biographical self has to be abstracted from that diversity."[5] In *The Truth of Poetry*, he began his discussion by calling attention to Pessoa as *the* modern poet of "multiple personality and self-division."[6] Himself a poet, Hamburger has also written what he calls "persona poems," especially a set of "early monologues."[7]

It is not immediately apparent that "Lisbon Night" is one of his "persona" poems. At first blush, it looks very much like the sort of lyric poem that might have been written by any traveler who is having trouble sleeping.

At one-thirty a.m. my friend gets through to me on the 'phone
To explain how he missed me at the hotel, I missed him at his
  flat,
And we make an appointment at last. The cacophonous throb
Of competing juke boxes in the pinball saloons has ended,
The cabarets down in the square have closed their doors.
Only motor bicycles rev and clatter; and all over the city
Still the twenty-one revolutions and counter-revolutions take
  place
On the walls. I begin to extract a silence, a privacy from
The repeated yap and whine of a dog in a nearby year,
When not later than two or two-thirty, long before dawn,
The false alarm clock, a denatured cock
Shrills, irresistibly shrills again and again,
Ripping me out of a quarter-sleep filled with the alleys,
The pine, eucalyptus, cedar and fish smells of Lisbon,
Glaze of tiled housefronts, the slippery marble of
    paving-stones,
Mountainside follies at Sintra that out-moored the Moors,
Conimbriga's Roman remains, the plastic and onion skins

That outshone sea-shells on the beaches at Foz-do-Douro—
Rich, inexhaustible cud for a drowsy mind.
Only dream could have done it, thoroughly pulping the stuff
For its own polymorphous needs, like taking me to a palace
To talk with Mozart in Portugal, then on, with him,
To a summer skiing resort in the Dutch Alps,
Where we're met by . . . But not now. There's nothing for it
But to live, as the poor do here, on credit, making the best
Of expecting the worst, and where other energy can't,
For the moment, be drawn upon, keep going on coffee.
Insomnia, television—they're much the same,
After all, apart from the missing knob.
So, resigned, I wait for the kinder blankness of morning.[8]

Hamburger dates his poem 1975, during the year following the military-led revolution of April 25 that toppled the long dictatorship of António Salazar and, at the end, Marcelo Caetano. The city's walls were still covered with graffiti, as the poem indicates, even as the new political freedoms expressed themselves in the formation of governments that lasted for weeks or even days. It is as if the English poet that Fernando Pessoa sometimes was had returned to Lisbon and now filed a kind of self-centered report as he was wont to do. Compare the opening lines of "Lisbon Revisited (1926)," the poem attributed to the Edinburgh-trained naval engineer Álvaro de Campos, himself a notable insomniac.

> Nothing holds me to anything.
> I want fifty things at the same time.
> With the anguish of one ravenous for meat, I yearn
> For something, I don't know what—
> Definitely for the indefinite . . .
> Restlessly asleep, I live in the restless dream-state
> Of one restlessly asleep, half in a dream.[9]

Or one can compare Hamburger's poem of a sleepless night in Lisbon with lines from Campos's 1929 poem entitled "Insomnia":

> I cannot sleep; I cannot read when I wake at night.
> I cannot write when I wake at night,

I cannot think when I wake at night—
Oh Lord, I cannot even dream when I wake at night!

Ah, the opium of being anyone else!
I do not sleep, I lie, a wakeful corpse, just feeling.
And my feeling is an empty thought.
Things that happened to me pass by, jumbled up,
—All those things which I regret and blame myself for—;
Things that have never happened to me pass by, jumbled up;
—All those things which I regret and blame myself for—;
Jumbled things, which are nothing, pass me by;
I regret even those, I blame myself for them, and I cannot sleep.

I have no strength of will to light a cigarette.
I stare at the opposite wall of my room as if it were the universe.[10]

Campos's "jumbled things"—thoughts, anguish, yearnings, shifting feelings—reemerge in Hamburger's poem. They show forth as the assorted details of both his daylight and dream life itineraries. And all this Hamburger sees with a modern, wasteful cast of whining dogs, denatured cocks, and poets who would be better off reading most of the night.

The English writer John Wain first published his poem "Thinking About Mr. Person" in the *New Lugano Review* in 1979. He identified his subject in a prefatory note: "Fernando Pessoa (1888-1935), a citizen of Lisbon, wrote four highly differentiated bodies of poetry, one under his own name (Pessoa, as it happens, means 'person') and the others under the names Alberto Caeiro, Ricardo Reis and Álvaro de Campos. A quiet, self-effacing man who published little, he enjoyed scant reputation in his lifetime, but is now widely regarded as 'the greatest Portuguese poet since Camões.'"[11] Wain's "long poem" (as it was described on both the cover and the contents page of the *New Lugano Review*) next appeared in 1980 as a chapbook. Accompanied by two etchings done by Bartolomeu dos Santos, it was published by the Chimaera Press, Beckenham, Kent. In the same year it was collected in *Poems, 1949-1979*, brought out in London by Macmillan. In 1981 the poem appeared in Portuguese translation. *Reflexões sobre o Sr. Pessoa*, translated by João Almeida Flor, with a note by Joaquim Manuel Magalhães, was published in Coimbra by Fenda Edições.

It is not clear when Wain first read the poetry of Pessoa and his heteronyms. He knew about the Portuguese poet at least by 1960, for in that year Wain reviewed the *Collected Poems of Roy Campbell*, the third volume of which included translations of three of Pessoa's orthonymic poems—"The thing that hurts and wrings," "Death comes before its time," and "The poet fancying each belief"—and of an excerpt from Álvaro de Campos's "Maritime Ode." "The bulk of the book," writes Wain, "consists of versions from the Spanish and Portuguese, and (still speaking personally) I read these with considerable enjoyment," for Campbell was "very well placed to translate Spanish and Portuguese poetry; he knew, and had shared, the way of life that underlay it, and he was more at home in that landscape than in green and rainy England."[12] Ten years later, he reviewed in *Encounter*—as part of an essay-review covering several books—Michael Hamburger's book *The Truth of Poetry*. Wain does not mention Pessoa, but one may suspect that something of Hamburger's lucid commentary and crisp analysis of the Portuguese poet's life and work lies behind Wain's general observation: "To be told about poet after poet, from country after country, to be shown examples of their work, to be introduced to their theories about poetry, and their views of the universe, and their personal circumstances, and the titles of their books, and the kind of thing they said in their letters, is to be (as another contemporary poet has put it) 'bombed with information.'"[13] Given the fact of Wain's own poem about Pessoa (more like a suite of interrelated poems), it is tempting to say that Hamburger's pages on Pessoa did not "bomb" so much as "seed." From Hamburger, Wain could have learned about Ricardo Reis and Alberto Caeiro, the two major heteronyms not represented in Campbell's translations in the third volume of *Collected Poems*, as well as more about the orthonymic Fernando Pessoa. The poetry Hamburger includes in his own translation are "Autopsicografia" and lines from Álvaro de Campos's poems, including "Ode Marítima." Significantly, the author-to-be of "Thinking About Mr. Person" (but already the author of even longer poems such as *Wildtrack, Letters to Five Artists*, and *Feng*) also takes issue with Edgar Allan Poe's notions concerning the impossibility of the "long poem."

Hamburger's essay heralded various demonstrations of interest in Pessoa in the early 1970s, when a few English-language translations appeared. In the ten years that separate Hamburger's book from Wain's "Thinking About Mr. Person," several worthy translations were published. The year 1971 saw, as indicated at the beginning of this book, the appearance of collections by four different translators emanating from as many presses. Carcanet brought out Jonathan Griffin's version of Pessoa, and Swallow published Edwin Honig's selection. Peter Rickard's sample appeared under the aegis of Edinburgh University Press, and the University of Wales Press published F.E.G. Quintanilha's sixty poems. In 1974 Jonathan Griffin's work was republished by Penguin.

"Thinking About Mr. Person" presents us with an inverted "Miniver Cheevy" or a serene "J. Alfred Prufrock," in which everything that E.A. Robinson chided in his subject and everything T.S. Eliot satirized in his have been transvalued when seen at work in the life of "Mr. Person." If Wain's subject is "less defined," he is also "less hampered." He is not Edgar Allan Poe's man of the crowd, a harried flaneur who cannot stand being alone; rather he is the creator of four poets who do his living for him, setting him free thereby "to enjoy being alone." Quieter than Whitman, who did not ask the overwhelming question "what is the self" because from the start he knew he contained multitudes, Mr. Person asks the question only to afford himself the opportunity to assert that he wants "no final choice / of mask or diagram / no sealed-in 'this I am': / needing his plural voice." Like Whitman (but unlike Miniver Cheevy) Mr. Person welcomes life, and like Whitman (but unlike Prufrock) he is happy to think about rivers. Whitman haunts this poem even as he haunts the poetry of Alberto Caeiro and Álvaro de Campos. The very idiom of the poem, a kind of "talking and questioning" that also recalls Pessoa's poetry (particularly that of Álvaro de Campos), is Whitman's invention, as Wain reveals elsewhere:

> Ah there, Walt! You invented this idiom,
> this kind of talking and questioning in a poem:
> and you were an old poet, too, in time,
> and people visited you in Camden, New Jersey:
> ah there, Walt! I have always loved you too.[14]

Besides its impressive literary genealogy, "Thinking About Mr. Person" evokes the atmosphere of Pessoa's Lisbon ("citizens with head colds riding in the trams, the yellow trams") and conveys the quotidian sense of Wain's own Portugal ("the long empty roads, the eucalyptus trees, / the rice fields and the Atlantic promontories"). This ordered sequence of images testifies to Wain's own original relationship to the country. In fact, Wain reveals that he chose Lisbon as the setting for his 1982 novel *Young Shoulders* (entitled *The Free Zone Stops Here* in the United States) because he was "so immersed in the atmosphere of Lisbon and so familiar with its layout."[15]

The evidence for thinking so is only circumstantial, but it is possible that there is an Oxford link between Wain's interest in Pessoa and that of another English writer-turned-translator of Mr. Person's poetry. In 1971 Wain became the first holder of the Fellowship in Creative Arts at Brasenose College. In 1973 he was elected professor of poetry. In the same year Andrew Harvey, born in India but educated in England, became a fellow of All Souls College. Wain's professional acquaintance with Harvey dates from no later than 1974, five years before the publication of Wain's poem about Pessoa when Wain and Harvey collaborated on a commercial tape in which they discussed Gerard Manley Hopkins's religious language in "The Wreck of the Deutschland." In 1977 Wain introduced Harvey's *Winter Scarecrow*, a book of poems. Two years later, in 1979, as editor of a collection entitled *An Edmund Wilson Celebration*, Wain solicited and published an original essay by Harvey.

In 1987 Andrew Harvey published translations of eighteen of Pessoa's poems in *Normal*, a New York quarterly of "Arts and Ideas." In his prefatory note Harvey obliquely acknowledges Wain's poem when he refers to Pessoa in passing as "Mr. Person":

Fernando Pessoa, with Rilke and Yeats, dominates twentieth-century poetry. Less visionary than Rilke and less brashly rhetorical than Yeats, he seems in many ways more contemporary in his range of acid bewilderments, his peculiar and plangent mixture of skepticism, anguish and bald detachment. Pessoa published only a handful of poems in his lifetime; the rest, more than three thousand, were found in neat stacks in a trunk after his death. Pessoa, which means "person" in Portuguese, wrote under three main "personae," each with their different "biographies" and "philosophies." Alberto Caeiro is a zen-like ascetic of the simple vision; Álvaro de Campos, a fervid romantic nihilist with suppressed homoerotic yearnings; Ricardo Reis, a stoic with a passion for stasis. Read separately, and then together, the works of these three personae throw constantly shifting light on the mystery that was, and is "Pessoa," "Mr. Person," the supreme actor of the Self, simultaneously absent and present in each of his impersonations of his own non-existence.[16]

The poems translated are by Pessoa's three major heteronyms: Campos, Caeiro, and Reis. There are five poems by Campos, nine by Caeiro, and six by Reis.[17] The orthonymic Pessoa is not represented.

Some of the lacks are notable. Besides excluding all poems by Pessoa himself (*êle-mesmo*), Harvey has also excluded, in his selection from Reis, all poems that address or name Neera, Chloe, or Lídia, the lovers whose names Reis took over from Horace and put to his own uses. In themselves, these omissions may not seem remarkable. Their omission, singly and together, would seem at first not to require further commentary. Their significance emerges when it is noticed that Harvey had already employed Pessoa himself (*êle-mesmo*) and Reis's Lídia in an earlier work. They are the bases for central figures named Fernando and Lydia in *No Diamonds, No Hat, No Honey*, a sequence of thirty-nine poems published in 1984.

In Pessoa's work Lídia appears only in Reis's poems. But Harvey changes that. He conceives of a Fernando, who is a writer, and a Lydia, who seems to be his confidant and, possibly, companion, though clearly not his pliant lover. She is a muse of reality, one who reinforces certain durable realities for Fernando by recalling his weaknesses, deflating his flights of rhetoric, calling him on his staged pronouncements, his pretentious opinions. Unlike Reis's Lídia, who never says a word, who sits there mutely before Reis's staged pronouncements, Harvey's Fernando's Lydia is nothing if not verbal. When Fernando begins his lament "By the waters of Babylon I sat down and . . . ," Lydia finishes his compound verb. "'Shat,' said Lydia loudly."[18] It is no better when Fernando implores. "'At

least I am honest,' I say. 'You'll give me that.'" Lydia replies:
"'Why should I give you anything? / Could Nebuchadnezzar not
eat grass?/ Could Jane Russell hide her breasts and ass?/ You
are what you are./ You are what you are condemned to be'"
(34). When he cries out: "'Balls,' I say, stroking her left thigh, /
'YOU get to me! You really do!'"—"'Say that again,' she says, 'it
always amuses me / When you do the sincerity bit. Wide eyes,
central vein staring'" (24). To Fernando with his wisdom showing, she teases, "'Say it all over, / I love it when you play the
sage. / There are so few true pleasures— / Why miss the way
your face/ Hardens to a mask and lies, and lies,/ When you talk
wise?'" (56). No wonder that, in these face-to-face encounters
with not a white goddess of poetry but the nagging termagant
that is his fate, Fernando sometimes gets "butch" (62).

At times Fernando claims to have invented his Lydia. He
wonders "'did Saul invent Her [the Witch of Endor], as I do you
/ To keep him company as his life goes bad?'" (37). Lydia is furi-
ous at this, her eyes "furnaces." "'No man,' she roared, 'entirely
invents his doom!'" (37).[19] Like Reis and his fictitious Lídia, this
Fernando and his Lydia are not really lovers. Yet this Fernando's
lover does seem to have a lover. As Lydia advises: "'Kill your ap-
plauding fool, you fool, / Pray every night / As you fall asleep in
his arms / You'll wake to find him dead / At the bottom of the
bed'" (34).

Harvey has imagined a relationship between Pessoa's fictitious characters that Pessoa had not explored or perhaps even
detected. It does not matter whether he has hooked up the orthonymic Pessoa with the imagined lover of the heteronymic
Reis or whether he has brought together the heteronymic
Pessoa himself (êle-mesmo) with the real Lídia whom his heteronymic Reis addresses in his poems. What does matter is that
Harvey, building ingeniously within Pessoa's world, adds a new
dimension to that world. Taking hints and leads in Pessoa's own
created personalities and spiriting them through his metrical
maze, Harvey has emulated brilliantly the novelistic experiment of José Saramago, whose *The Year of the Death of Ricardo
Reis* (*O ano da morte de Ricardo Reis*) carries on that last heteronym's life beyond that of his creator.

The poet Dennis Silk turns a similar trick on a small scale, this time imagining a gripe session in which Pessoa's three major heteronyms confront their creator. Born in London in 1928 and a resident of Israel since 1955, Silk is the author of four collections of poetry: *A Face of Stone* (1964), *The Promised Land* (1980), *Hold Fast* (1984), and *Catwalk and Overpass* (1990). To honor Edwin Honig on his seventy-fifth birthday, this Anglo-Israeli poet offered his tribute in the form of a poem entitled "Mandive House":

Self-pondering heteronyms arrive at their parent: Fernando Pessoa.
Raymond Zar—he is about to name a figment. They catch him
red-handed.
Álvaro de Campos says: I might have been Mr. Manticula, and happy,
but you made me into a rowdy engineer.
Alberto Caeiro says he dislikes to figure in pastoral.
Nonplussed Pessoa looks down at flowing Tagus. Still, he mutters,
I'm Fernando the Only. Or, Ricardo Reis returns, only Fernando.[20]

It is not a figure in one of the poems (as is the case with Harvey's Lydia) who gets on Fernando's case in Silk's poem, but the major heteronyms themselves. Two of them complain that their au-thor has determined their fate in less than happy ways. In "Mandive House" Silk invokes a principle of human personality and character defined figurally in "Under the Weather," a poem in *The Punished Land:*

Men are changed by the things they carry. A sheet of glass,
and a man is a glazier. That's undeniable.

Here's the packet-man tying himself up. He never once addressed himself to the muse of string.

Or the shoe-shine boy who never got out of the polish. He's in
disarray. What does he do when he looks into the shine?

A hat brim lifted a man. What will become of me?[21]

Campos can no more cease being an engineer than the shoe-shine boy can escape his polish, and Caeiro will forever figure in the pastoral that gives him being. If the stoical, supercilious

Reis will not stoop to whining, he will disguise his complaint as an observation that shrinks Pessoa to human size. Pessoa's "Fernando the Only" is, alas, Reis's "only Fernando." To which one might counter, "True enough, but his measure is that at one and the same time, he manages to be both."

Appendix

Roy Campbell's *Fernando Pessoa*

Editor's Note: Errors of fact and misspellings have been neither corrected nor flagged. Substantive deletions have been recorded in notes, while negligible changes, slips of the pen, and false starts have not. In two or three instances, Campbell crossed out large sections of his manuscript with a single stroke. But these deletions, in my opinion, do not constitute revisions of his text. They indicate a secondary use of material and as such are indications of what must be excised temporarily so that the unmarked material might be used for some other purpose. If my reading is accurate in this respect, such temporarily excluded material would eventually have been restored to its original place in the text of his book on Pessoa.

Fernando Pessoa

1. An Elusive Personality

When, in 1910, I first went to the Durban High School (Preparatory) I was eight years old, but I can still remember the name "F. Pessoa," which was carved on the under-side of the liftable lid of my desk.[1] The lowest form in the school naturally inherited the most ancient and time-worn desks, while the new desks were issued to the higher forms in the upper school. From the look of it, this desk must have been in use for fifteen years. It was carved and cut about by half a generation of schoolboys. Though a mere coincidence, the fact that so many years ago, and so many thousand miles away, I once sat on the same seat as Pessoa, makes me feel nearer to my "enigmatic" subject, *personally* nearer to him, if one could ever use such a word in deal-

108

ing with the most elusive and impersonal of poets. At least I have a personal proof of his existence, of his human existence, as a schoolboy wasting his time, in the usual way, by spoiling a desk: and also wishing to perpetuate his name. Most schoolboys are content with carving their initials. Ironically enough, the word Pessoa means *person*. Yet though Pessoa could project vivid personalities and temperaments under the three different heteronyms of the fictitious poets, *Álvaro dos Campos, Ricardo Reis,* and *Alberto Caeiro,* each with a style and character of his own, whom he invented as Shakespeare invented his almost superhuman characters, Pessoa, himself, remains as shadowy and impersonal in his own signed, best work, as Shakespeare, himself, remains in *his.*

I have known the friends of his childhood in South Africa, notably Mr. Ormond of Durban, his closest schoolfriend, with whom he corresponded for twenty years, and for whom he preserved a feeling almost akin to affection,[2] although he lapsed from the Catholicism in which his friend staunchly continues. (Pessoa was highly conscious of his Jewish ancestry on one side). My father was the family doctor of the Pessoas in Durban. I have known countless friends and acquaintances of his maturity, who comprise most of the poets and artists in Portugal, who were old enough to take part in the literary and bohemian life of Lisbon up to the date of his death, in 1935. Yet it is extremely difficult to obtain any clear outlines of his character, or any salient anecdotes about his life, from anyone who knew him. On the subject of his life, his four different voices, so contradictory on all other themes, are in complete agreement concerning this one enigma. The three voices which he ventriloquised from his inmost being, the three personalities he invented, the three poets he created by projecting them centrifugally from within, on this one subject, coincide with the one impersonal, involved, centripetal poet, whom he did not invent or create, but *was;* though, of course, in the long run, he *was* the other three, too. *Alberto Caeiro,* who was the least complex, in style and thought, of Pessoa's fourfold team, was also, in his creator's opinion, the most straightforward and sincere of the four. (Pessoa held that absolute sincerity was incompatible with art yet he tried to create a genuinely sincere poet in *Alberto Caeiro*).

Alberto Caeiro writes thus, concerning his biographical future:

> If, when I die, they wish to write my life—
> Why, nothing could be simpler;
> It only has two dates . . . my Birth and Death.
> What comes between, belongs to me alone.

Even *Álvaro dos Campos*, the rip-roaring, extroverted, often hysterical, rampaging, Whitman-yawping *dos Campos*, who seems to be Pessoa's extrovert reaction against his own timid, introverted self—seems to change his positiveness to evasive negation, when dealing with this one theme, and to fall into line with his crepuscular father, and undemonstrative brethren, the coldly classical *Reis*, and the reserved puritan *Caeiro*. Biographically, *dos Campos*, who is a cross between Marinetti and Whitman, wishes no more than

> To be sheer nought, like figures in romances,
> Without material death, life, or ideas:
> Not utilised nor blemished, but to be as
> Shadows on unreal ground, or dreams in trances.

Ricardo Reis, the morose, coldly Augustan, member of the team, agrees in turn.

> Like a rich burden, glory overloads us.
> Fame, like a fever, burns.
> Love tires—because it's serious in its searching.
> Knowledge—none ever learns.
> Passing, Life hurts, because it knows all this.
> Life, like a game of chess,
> Grips our whole soul; but, lost, it weighs but little;
> And, after, even less!

Then we hear Pessoa, himself, summing up in a letter, and, for once, almost explaining himself:

"For the rest, my life revolves entirely around my literary work, good or bad . . . Everything else in life has for me but a secondary importance[.]"

The selection of these four quotations by my friend Dr João Gaspar Simões, with which to prelude his monumental edition of "The Life and Work of Fernando Pessoa,"[3] was a wise precaution, which he recommended me to follow as an excuse for, and an explanation of the lack of biographical matter. In answer to the legitimate curiosity of so many enthusiastic readers,[4] one can only refer to the above quotations[.] Gaspar Simões, who knew Pessoa better than most people, at first set out to collect all the testimonies available (from friends, acquaintances, old schoolfriends, journalistic colleagues, relatives, patrons, and even café-waiters, who knew Pessoa) so as to reconstruct the "drama" of Pessoa's life, "within whose framework was spun the work which constitutes his immortal tie with this world." In his previous work on Portugal's greatest prose writer, and novelist, Eça de Queiroz, Dr Simões had reconstructed a dynamic and unforgettable "drama." At first, he hoped to repeat the feat in the case of Portugal's greatest poet since Luis de Camões. He had to give up the idea, with the feeling that Pessoa's poetry was rather the immortal tie of his *terrestrial incarnation* to this world, "since it was never his Mother-Country, nor was he ever an acclimatised native of it." He left scarcely a fingerprint, apart from his letters, and his work. In spite of the fact that Pessoa died only 15 years before Gaspar Simões wrote his book, the latter rightly says it would be a thousand times easier to evoke the existence of almost anyone who had died two hundred years ago. "Therefore," says the Doctor, "I have trusted exclusively to the obvious and only possible testimony for such a biography— the testimony of written documents and letters": from these it is possible to raise a figure which is independant alike of the reticences of[5] those who fear to tell what they know: and from the fantasy of those[6] whose ostentation claims to know more than anyone else, or who can only speak about themselves, when asked about someone else.

From this, and from the quotations I made above, it is obvious that we are face to face with a purely literary poet, like Valery, Rilke or Mallarmé, a man, yes, but a man to whom, as in the case of Keats, literature was food, drink, work, recreation, repose, religion, life itself, and after-life immortality as well. Such a man can only be evoked through his written work and his letters, yet, even here, there is an unsoundable gulph. We

have nearly all Keats's letters, and they have been the inspiration and the standby of many biographers. Fortunately, Pessoa
was a great letter-writer, but his longest and finest correspondence, to judge from the replies they evoked from the fine poet,
Mario de Sá Carneiro, was lost when the latter committed
suicide in 1916 at the Hotel de Nice in Paris. The Portuguese
Consul, Senhor Carlos Alberto Ferreira, remembers going
through Sá Carneiro's pockets and his trunk, after the suicide,
and seeing in the trunk a huge packet of letters from Pessoa: but
the trunk and its contents had to be retained against the pay-
ment of Sá Carneiro's enormous hotel bill, and when it was finally sought, years afterwards, the management had changed
hands, and all was lost. The pathetic thing about it was that Sá
Carneiro, in his half of this correspondence, envisaged the publication "in 1950" of Pessoa's letters to him, which he was keeping for that purpose—and the triumphant success of the publication! As Sá-Carneiro's half of the correspondence amounts to
more than two hundred letters, and since we can guess, from
his reactions, the intellectually stimulating and inspiring quality of Pessoa's letters, one can judge what a loss has befallen
European literature through the loss of Sá Carneiro's trunk.
Though Carneiro had not the *stature*, the volume, nor the
grandeur of Pessoa, he was a poet of the highest *quality*, in his
more limited sphere: and both of these poets had a greater influence on each other than was had by any of their contemporaries on each other, or on either of them.

Pessoa called his heteronymous creations a "drama in
people," and invented somewhat summary biographies to tack
on to each of his heteronyms. He even wrote letters to and from
them, and from them to each other, to heighten their reality. But
as Adolfo Casais Monteiro points out in his "Fernando Pessoa
and His Critics," the biography in each case was written, and
the poets were invented, to suit the poetry—which is Pessoa's:
instead of the poetry being written to suit the fictitious poets of
the heteronymous drama. We must not lose sight of this fact as
the Academic critics did,[7] whom Casais Monteiro, a considerable polemist, rebukes so very amusingly.

Pessoa (even without his heteronymous creation) would
probably be the greatest Portuguese poet since Camões (with
the possible exception of the nineteenth Century poet, Antero

de Quental) but whereas Camões' life, like that of his contemporaries Ercilla, Lope, and Cervantes was a series of mountainous adventures, such as would have sprained the imagination of our mere modern Munchausens, Dr Charles M. Doughty, or his disciple, T.E. Lawrence, the self-styled "Prince of Mecca," and his colourful stage-manager, Mr. Lowell Thomas, and Captain Liddell Hart—the life of Pessoa hardly exists outside the covers of his books, or the envelopes of his letters. Yet as an expert in mystification, Pessoa resembles Lawrence, and excels him. Yet it is difficult for us not to believe in the authenticity of *Álvaro dos Campos* as a hard-living, much-travelled, adventurous, seafaring naval engineer, educated in England, and wearing a monocle,—even when we know his origin in the imagination of Pessoa. Physically, though not in temperament, *Álvaro dos Campos* took after his creator. He was "vaguely of the typical build of the Portuguese jew," slightly round-shouldered, with a stoop, and a complexion between sallowness and pallor. There is a certain ostentatious arrogance about him. He is sensual, cruel, callous, and violent at the same time. So much more effective is poetry than the most sensational form of advertisement on the most Colossal scale, that the fictitious creation of poetry remains untouched by our knowledge of its origin, and *Álvaro dos Campos* lives for us: whereas the pretentious cabotinage of a Lawrence, though supported by National Policy, launched by million-dollar movie-and-press campaigns, backed up by Fleet Street, the BBC, by all the prime-ministers, bemedalled Marshalls, literary pundits, and titled diplomatists who first fell into his booby-trap, and do not wish to look fools now—wilts, crumbles, and vanishes the moment we know the origin of the myth or the legend, in the brain of an American journalist. Yet when we know the origin of the legendary *Álvaro dos Campos, Ricardo Reis,* and *Alberto Caeiro,* in the mind of a poet, we marvel all the more! It makes no difference that they are inventions, since their performance is so absolutely real, their achievement so far beyond doubt.

2. "O Menino da sua Mãe" (His Mother's Pet-Boy)

The early environment of Fernando Pessoa influenced his imagery so profoundly that it is worth recording. He was born at

number 4 in the Largo, or Square, of Saint Carlos, then a kind
of municipal backwater, off the Chiado, which is "the Bond
street of Lisbon," on the 13th of June 1888. Contemporary pho-
tographs bear out his description of São Carlos square, as a
"village square," though one side of that square is entirely oc-
cupied by the Grand Opera House of São Carlos, the main en-
trance of which is exactly opposite the door of his birthplace.
In those days of hansoms and buggies, grass grew in the
middle of the square. Today it is one of the busiest car-parking
grounds in Lisbon: the wonderful view which the Pessoas got
from their top window has been completely blocked out by
taller buildings erected since then. In 1880, however, the Largo
de São Carlos gave the illusion of being a "village square" in the
heart of a great city, with a magnificent marine panorama of
the Atlantic horizon and the Tagus full of towering sails,
"where Neptune reigns so far inland," to quote from that
breath-taking passage of Tirso de Molina in "El Burlador de
Sevilla," wherein the Commendador describes, to the King of
Spain, the view from the Misericordia of Lisbon, which is quite
near the Largo de Saint Carlos, and would not differ very
greatly in Tirso's time from what it was in Fernando Pessoa's
time—since that part of the City which was altered by the in-
tervention of the Earthquake in the Eighteenth Century, is
more or less "dead ground," and invisible from the summit
above. This famous passage of Tirso's is one of the finest in all
Renaissance literature; in its detail and grandeur it resembles a
Breughel picture. A rough translation of Tirso's verbal picture,
and of his innate perception of the glorious aims of Portuguese
imperialism before the decadence, which is implicit in every
line of his picture—will give a better idea of the surroundings
of Pessoa's high-swung cradle, than I could give in prose. If the
galleons and galleys of Tirso's description are lacking today,
they are made up for, and, at a brief distance, indistinguishable
from, the towering sails of the cod-fishing fleet, on its annual
setting forth and return, to and from the shores of Nova Scotia,
Newfoundland, and Labrador. The smaller sloops, chasse-
marées, and lateen-sailed fishing boats are there, without any
innovations or changes: and the whole panorama lights up in
one's memory as one reads it in the "Trickster of Sevilla." Of
course, in 1888, Lisbon harbour was still full of four-masted

clippers, and would resemble Tirso's description even more than it does today.

The poet seems to have retained throughout his forty-seven years of life an indelible memory of this panorama, which forms the background of so many of his finest poems: but very soon afterwards that majestic view was unobtainable from any part of that quarter of Lisbon. As Pessoa writes, regretfully,

It was in the old quiet house by the river . . .
The dining room windows and those of my room
Overlooked the low buildings, and gave on the nearby river,
On the Tagus, this very same Tagus, but much lower down.
Were I to arrive at those windows now, they would not be those
     windows at all.
That time has passed like the smoke of a steamer upon the high seas.

His father died when he was five years old. He seems to have regarded his father and mother with the greatest tenderness, and to have thought of his early childhood, in the Largo de São Carlos, as a lost paradise: for, whenever he refers to it in his verse, the lines become either poignant or rapturous. Dr Gaspar Simões says the five years that passed between his birth and the death of his father remained like an "indefinable melody" in his imagination. Within twenty yards of his cradle the great bells of the Church of Martyrs (where he was baptised), "dolente na tarde calma," sounded "mournfully in the calm evening," and at night the half-heard music of Verdi and Wagner would rise up beneath the stars, from the Opera, enchanting his wondering childhood with strange, vague sounds; while the winds from the orange-blossoms on the Cintra mountains to the North, or the rosemary-scented crags of the Arràbida to the South, would come straight to his windowsill, at the central summit of the town, without any interruption, till they drooped, died, and trailed down into the lower, sweating, narrow streets of the city beneath, and the coal-dusty shipping at its base. The country air, up there, gave Pessoa's "village square" an extra illusion of being in the country. The same year as Fernando's father died, a baby brother was born, thus isolating the future poet from his parents. His fifth birthday was the saddest day of his life, for it was forgotten in the birth of his brother, and the impending death of his father, who expired shortly after in the arms of his very beautiful wife. The Pessoas had been a purely military family till Joaquim, the poet's father, the son of a general, became a journalist and evinced a taste for music and letters. His mother, Dona Madalena Pinheiro Nogueira, came from the Ilha Terceira (or Third Island) of the Azores, where her family was one of the most distinguished. Almost simultaneously beset by the death of a husband and the birth of a child, Dona Madalena had to abandon Fernando to the care of an aunt and two old servants, who were very deep in peasant lore and fascinated him with their ballads, tales, and songs.

But Dom Joaquim had left his family badly off. His death was followed by a sale of furniture, and the removal of the whole family to poorer lodgings, further from the river, with hardly any view at all. These lodgings were in the Rua de São Marçal: and into these very much smaller rooms, the widowed mother of the poet had to cram herself, her two small sons, two maids, and a crazy paternal grandmother. The younger child died shortly after, and Fernando was restored to the first and only place in his mother's heart. He became almost too much of a "mother's boy": and being sensitive and precocious, all his tenderness and affection was monopolised and returned by his mother. There is a wonderfully profound play by Calderon de la Barca, called "Eco y Narciso," which shows the effect of too much mother-love on a youth in isolating him from his fellow men, and effeminising him. The result is Narcissus suicidally in love with himself. Most of what we call panzies are the result of too much motherly protection: but the latinised celtiberian temperament does not effeminize so easily as the Saxon. Speaking of the work of his one dear friend, Mario Sá Carneiro, Fernando Pessoa said, "it is full of an intimate inhumanity . . . it has no human warmth, no human tenderness, because he lost his mother when he was two years old, and never properly knew maternal tenderness." The first poem Pessoa ever wrote, was to his mother, and his case may be said to have been, at first, the inverse of that of his closest friend, Sá Carneiro. Fear of his crazy grandmother, when she had her mad fits, during which she became dangerous and had to be locked up, drove him to clutch his mother's skirts even more closely. Fear seconded love in attaching him to the apron strings. In her mad moments, children were the beings his

grandmother hated most in the world. The intellectual development of Fernando Pessoa began so early that he knew the
vowels when he was eight months old. Being so impressionable at such an early age, it is small wonder that this early fear
of his mad grandmother tinged his whole later attitude to life,
with a haunting fear: at the same time the sensitive child felt
an aching, overwhelming homesickness for the old house in
the "village square." Both this fear, and this nostalgia enlaced
him so inextricably in the apron strings of his mother, that the
ties grew tighter with time, and outlasted his forty-seven years
of life, though she, for her part, broke away from them soon, in
a second marriage[.] The haunting sadness and fear of Pessoa's
own later poems must have been indelibly printed on his character at this time: and I feel that the poems of *Álvaro dos
Campos*, and the fiction of their fiery author, was a desperate
attempt on the part of Fernando Pessoa to free himself imaginatively from the apron-strings that tethered him in real life,
so long after his mother had released herself from them. He
may have learned from his mad grandmother, in her kindly,
quieter moments, as she sat muttering in a corner, to create
and people a world of his own, which would be independant of
this world and its restrictions. At any rate, he was only six
when he created his first imaginary companion, a certain
"Chevalier de Pas" to whom he wrote, actually posting the letters to the care of his own address: and whom he caused to
reply to him, by writing and posting the "Chevalier's" letters
back to himself.

In this we are reminded of the Brontës who populated their
bleak isolation with fictitious authors of their own poems. This
creation of fictitious friends and correspondents (for there
were, shortly, many more than the "Chevalier de Pas") coincides
with the appearance on the scene of his future step-father who
was to share but not to alienate entirely the attention of
Fernando's beautiful and lively Mother. "His mother's Pet-Boy"
had to become "his own pet boy," to compensate for the affection that was switched on to his rival, and, eventually, his
master, though a kind one.

The poet, later, was to write this unexpected confession. "I
have verified that those who have had step-parents in life are
always lacking in affection, whether they are artists or merely

simple men—whether they lost their mother through death, through coldness and indifference, or through her affections having been diverted by someone else. Those who lost their mothers by death, always turn their affection on to themselves as a substitute for their unknown mother: those who have lost their mothers through coldness, indifference, or the diversion of their affections—become implacable cynics, and monstrous offspring of the natural love that has been denied them." There is a touch of self-pity in this. Here, he is referring to, and exaggerating, his own case. Pessoa did not "lose his mother through death." He didn't even lose her at all: there was only a slight deflection of her entire care and attention. But he felt the loss of what she shared with another, very deeply, since he had once monopolised the whole of her care. There is also a parallel to this in Baudelaire who was spiritually wounded, almost maimed, by the second marriage of his mother, and often had cruelly cynical moods. So having felt himself for a whole year, the most impressionable year of his life, as being the entire, sole object of his mother's love[8] and attention, the loss of even half of that attention affected Pessoa as violently as a death would have affected a child in a more normal situation. If it did not make him an implacable cynic and a monster, it made him to quote Gaspar [Simões], "that frigid mistificator, that sort of impersonal, timeless, and abstract theatre-stage, upon which the strange tragicomedy of his poetic creation was about to commence."

There is more than a slight Cagliostro strain in Pessoa's character. Mystification, deception, and sadism are almost invariably the refuge or compensation in disappointed Narcissi or "Mothers-boys." The Author of "the Mint" or, as I call it, "the Bint,"[9] though not comparable as a writer, was almost Pessoa's equal in the art of mystification: but he revels and gloats in the sadistic description of the decomposition of a beautiful woman's body in the panzie song about the death of Queen Alexandra from syphilis. There is an equally gloating strong sadistic strain in the bloodthirsty piratical passage of Pessoa in the *Maritime Ode*. The difference was that, though both Pessoa and Lawrence were dreamers, Pessoa satisfied his sadism[10] harmlessly in his day-dreams.[11] The more sinister Lawrence got a real chance to satisfy his criminal instincts in his unsoldierly killing and torturing of his Turkish prisoners, and of the women virgins and children of Damascus and other towns, whom he set his Arabs on to rape and torture though incapable of raping them himself through being a "queer." Still there is a very strong parallel to Pessoa in T.E. Lawrence. And there is the same bone freezing callousness—"then we turned the Hotchkiss on to the prisoners and made an end of them" (*Seven Pillars of Moonshine.*) This might be out of *Ode Maritima*.

Pessoa's lack of heart-felt comradeship or affection (except in the case of Sá Carneiro and a shadowy woman friend,[12] who prefers to remain anonymous, and keep his letters unpublished during her life-time) is the reason why he remains almost incognito, personally, to the many people who "knew" him, knew that he was a great poet, wire-electrified by his conversation, and impressed enough by his poetry to become his patrons. His friendships with Sá Carneiro and Ormond were chiefly *intellectual*, though lasting. When people part with money it means they recognise a genius, if not a person. They want fame which is one of the worthiest aims in life next to spiritual salvation. Again, here, we are reminded of that other great heartless mystifier T.E. Lawrence, the greatest mystery-merchant of the age, next to Pessoa himself. Lawrence, too, who had a grievance against his mother, and sought foster-mothers everywhere amongst elderly ladies (for he was a savage misogynist and sadist where younger women were concerned) till he found one, in Mrs Bernard Shaw. There is the same bone-freezing callousness to human feeling in Lawrence: but in Pessoa's case it is mental: there is not the brutal physical cynicism of the sadistic[13] Lawrence,[14] with his Arabs always skulking in the rear of any dangerous action, shunning any real fighting, and then torturing and flaying the wounded and Lawrence getting his Arabs on to rape and [pillage?] in Damascus. There is none of the actual[15] cruelty of the sadistic chorus to the "geste" of Lawrence's catamite army—"then we turned the Hotchkiss on the prisoners and made an end of them." Pessoa's sadism is imaginary. He dreams it. Lawrence acts it. How the English, having made a national hero of this wildly theatrical and hysterical rearguard hyaena, could have the hypocrisy to bump off German Generals, who did far less in that way, and only reluctantly, under dire necessity—is a mystery. By the same standards of judgement, what would have happened to Lawrence had [he] been a German criminal instead of a British one, and were he to have been hauled up at Nuremberg. He would have been the first to be hanged as a cowardly butcher of wounded, and women, and children. The[16] gyppos nightie that covers such a multitude of sins for a public that was reared on Rudolf Valentino, and never forgot it, would be despised by the other, greater expert in mystification, Fernando Pessoa, for his mystifications were[17] innocent. The difference between the two greatest Cagliostros and mystery-merchants of this Century, Fernando Pessoa and T.E. Lawrence, is that Pessoa's victories were real and valid in the shape of poems: and that he put himself and his heteronyms across without the aid of journalists and propaganda and the War Office, *unofficially*. Also Lawrence relied on artificial, theatrical aids such as "that gyppo's nightie" and that golden dagger, which for a public that had been reared on Rudolf Valentino (whom he copied) covered a multitude of sins. Pessoa's Cagliostro-acts were masterly, unaided, amusing, and creative—they generally add to and seldom diminish, his stature founded, as it is, on immortal achievements. He would have despised using fancy-dress; and as for the Press, he was not the spoilt darling of its publicity, but its Enemy Number One.[18] Casais Monteiro laughs at the fact that, even after his death, the great mystifier, Pessoa, could thoroughly pull the leg of his generous and great-hearted biographer, Dr Gaspar [Simões], who has some of that innocence that makes the devotion possible, with which he compiled his two monumental volumes, without which neither Casais Monteiro's amusing polemics could have happened, nor could such studies as this be made by foreign writers like myself. Gaspar Simões' volumes are a goldmine of inexhaustible wealth. If he tricked his best biographer at unguarded moments, Pessoa often mystified himself, and may yet mystify Casais Monteiro. He walked straight into his own booby-trap in his adventures with the fatuous imposter, Aleister Crowley, the diabolist, dogmatic immoralist, sadist, and black-magic expert: and if I had not (in complete ignorance of Pessoa's dealings with this idiotic monster) shortened the latter's stay in Portugal, in my role[19] of an *epater de bohemiens*, by planting a pair of explosive banderillas in his enormous posterior on the cliffs at Cascais, so that he beat an ignominious retreat home to England where he had to lie doggo for fear of ridicule, and to sleep face-downward for weeks—God only knows to what lengths of credulous self-mystification Pessoa might not have gone! This misfortune to Crowley explains the mysterious hiatus in Gaspar [Simões'] account of the Pessoa-Crowley affair. Pessoa affected a cynical, mephistophelean dandyism—the shabby dandyism of the modern penniless bohemian. There is a magnificent portrait of him by Almada Negreiros today in one of the Cafés ("Irmãos Unidos" in the Square of Rossio) where he spent so much of his life. This portrait not only brings out his mephistophelean dandyism—but almost a family likeness to the great actor, Charlie Chaplin, of which he seems an emaciated and elongated edition, with the same Jewish expression. It is a curious thing that the two greatest mystery merchants and "mothers' boys" of their age, the two most introverted egotists of our time, Pessoa and T.E. Lawrence, closely resembled two of the most famous clowns and comedians. If Pessoa was the elongated double of Charlie Chaplin whom he resembled even in the length of his feet (they are crossed in the above-mentioned portrait)—T.E. Lawrence was the doppelganger of another famous comedian, the "very spit" of Stan Laurel, of Laurel and Hardy—with Lowell Thomas as a sort of etherialised Hardy (on diet) in the background. But Portugal may thank God that Pessoa could mystify and trick himself. Like almost all the intellectuals of this century Pessoa accepted the regulation, stereotyped political[20] uniform of a masonico-liberaloid outlook, which is regarded by its wearers as a panacea for the disease that is rotting the world—rather than what it really is, one of the most alarming *symptoms* of that very disease. Pessoa like our own poets of the 'teens and twenties of this century was, at one time, dogmatically decadent and a-moral, though it was platonic and theoretical. He read Max Nordau's "Degeneration," as a sort of inverted Bible and he enjoyed Lombroso, the Freud and Jung of the nineties, just as Auden today takes Freud for a sort of

Talmud on which to found his *aesthetic,* his philosophy, and his conduct. The subordination of philosophy and poetry to science is responsible for the *hollow unreality* which underlies a lot of modern poetry, especially the bloodthirsty Fee-Fo-Fumming of the thirties.[21] Nearly all of the finest poets of the age have willingly subordinated their poetry to current scientific clap-trap, even Dylan Thomas and D.H. Lawrence who, in a sense, were deeply religious in spite of the fact that, in order to subordinate the moral to the a-moral, Freud had to subordinate the normal reality of working life to *the Dream.* It is through the Dream that Freud interprets living reality. The traditional rôle of the poet is to be wide awake, a defender and a builder and defender of civilization. It is only during the last century that poets have been enlisted as a "fifth-column" of underminers and demolishers in the service of technology and empirical science, which is not only demolishing civilization, but[22] systematically supersedes itself as Freud supersedes[23] Nordau and Lombroso and as they superseded[24] the phrenologists (once the last word in infallibility) who came before them. Pessoa though he was reared on Nordau and Lombroso, was a true Freudian because he subordinated real life to the dream: but by the time Freud became truly fashionable, amongst literary folk, Pessoa had become, like Yeats, preoccupied with occultism, theosophy, table rapping for spooks, Rosicrucianism, and that strange sort of dabbling with spells and enchantments which still persists amongst the educated Portuguese, who were too-suddenly disoriented by Masonic persecution from their hereditary creed. One sees the same thing in disoriented Irishmen, Conan Doyle and Yeats—they looked on Christianity as a superstition, yet there was no limit to their credulity wherever ectoplasm, planchettes, or cardboard trumpets were concerned. The practice of occultism and spiritualism seems to be almost inseparable from a certain amount of pretense and humbug, and it is difficult to set a dividing line where it leaves off. Pessoa camouflaged the dividing line with whimsical Portuguese humour. It is impossible to make out whether he was really as terrified of the black magician Crowley as he pretended to be. Crowley was a shallow fat-head and a terrible poltroon as I proved when I stuck the fire banderillas in his posterior and he went bucking like a bronco, and squealing like a pig, all over the cliffs of Cascais to the sound of loud squibs exploding and the laughter of Ruy Diaz and myself.

Confronted by the Freud of his time, who was Leon Hebreu, the traditional poet, in this case Ronsard, who was conscious of his functions and duties as a high priest of European culture, could place his trust in exactly the right spot, and drive back the interloper to within the narrow corral of the most rabidly racial culture the world has ever known, which, fanatically, resisting any encroachment from without, is nevertheless eternally and persistently encroaching onto and undermining the European civilization on which it fattens. Ronsard wrote of Leon Hebreu:

> Je crois qu'en luy coupant la peau de sa prepuce—
> On luy couper le coeur et toute affection.

He also wrote a prophetic poem, of the rôle played by Geneva in the destruction of Europe. Had the poets of the nineteenth and twentieth centuries done their duty, nobody would ever have heard of Marx, Freud, or Einstein, and the Atom Bomb would not exist outside the covers of the "Penny-Dreadfuls," where it belongs. There is no doubt that Psychoanalysis has acted on the noble White Man of the North West of Europe (and his literature), as the fire-water acted on the noble Red man of Europe. Had Freud and his army of healers come to spread and infect the whole race with the ailments in which they specialise (not to alleviate them, as they professed) they could not have spread them more effectively. The result of the subordination of real life to the dream, has been that for half a century most of the poets of Europe have been concerned with what was either politically or morally unreal: that is to say Utopias and Vices. It does not require much knowledge of biology, history, or theology to know that this is heading for racial destruction, suicide, or slavery. On this point, those three sciences concur—whether the agent of destruction be an earthquake, a plague, an eruption as in the case of Sodom and Gomorrah, or a conquistador like Cortés or Pizarro in which form destruction came to the inert Incas and Aztecs, or merely a quiet little professor with a dreamy expression and a neat little violin handy, on which to fiddle, when it goes up in flames!

Pessoa proved too smart for himself and contradicted his own liberaloid and masonic ideals—in the paradox of his sincere patriotism and in becoming, unconsciously, the prophet of the renascence of Portuguese imperialism under Salazar in a sense which would have made Kipling envious, though he sang in the century when his British Empire had received its mortal wounds from the South Africans, the Irish, and finally from Churchill's cringing policy of panic-stricken appeasement at all costs. The Portuguese empire has survived the British and the French empires because it was founded on a spiritual not a commercial basis. Camões was to the Portuguese Empire what Virgil was to the Roman,—the voice of imperialism. But Pessoa as the author of *Mensagem* will everlastingly be coupled with the author of *The Lusiads* as the voice of the Christian, Catholic imperialism of Portugal (though he hated Catholicism with all the hatred of a twentieth century intellectual, an occultist, and, moreover, of a devout masonico-Rosicrucian). *Mensagem* amounts to a marine Epic (written in short lyrics instead of six-line verses like *The Lusiads*). It is much finer than the terrific hundred-page *Maritime Ode* which he wrote under the name of *Álvaro dos Campos*, but spoilt with sadism, echoes of Stevensonian heartiness, and too much "Yo-ho-hoing." The irony of Pessoa's blossoming forth as a good Portuguese (under the Salazar regime!!) is to be attributed to his being haunted by the sails and the steamers seen in early childhood, and that beautiful panorama of the Tagus harbour at which one can gaze forever. He has to become, imaginatively, a sailor: the more he becomes a sailor the more he becomes a Portuguese, and a patriotic one. For a moment the blood of generations of his Portuguese soldier-ancestors overpowers the[25] cosmopolitan Jewish blood of which he had more than a shot in his veins. Here we must take a backward view of Portuguese military and naval history to show that the "heroics" of *Mensagem* are no idle day dream.[26] A lie was circulated during World War Number One, to the effect that the Portuguese made poor, cowardly soldiers. The author of this myth was the very general whom the Portuguese showed up (though very poorly equipped) by hanging on, twice, to sectors from which the British retired on the Western Front. Wellington, the greatest British soldier that ever lived (since not one of the adversaries crushed by Marlborough could come up to the knees of Soult, Ney, Massena, or Marmont, let alone Napoleon himself!) had such a high opinion of the Portuguese soldier that he used the Portuguese cavalry under Sir Benjamin D'Urban, the godfather of the City of Durban, as his spear-head on his advance up the Tagus. The Portuguese infantry shared the honours of the storming of Ciudad Rodrigo, Badajoz, and San Sebastian with the British, if they also shared the blame of the atrocities which followed. They contributed their share to the glorious victories of Talavera, Salamanca, Vitoria, Albuera, Vimeiro, El Bodon, the Nive, and the Nivelles, and the equally glorious drawn-fights of Fuentes de Oñoro, and Toulouse, which were really victories, *if judged by their results*. I was often in action with the Portuguese against the best troops on the Red side in the Spanish war, the Germans of the Thielmann Brigade, who finally formed the Nucleus of the Haganah and the Stern Gang, terrific fighters, who gave the British such a rough time in Palestine: and also against the Abraham Lincoln Brigade, tough, intelligent, and wily fighters—for there was a jolly sight more of Abraham than Lincoln, in that Brigade! The Portuguese volunteers were equal to both in Spain. Byron, in his *Childe Harold*, encouraged the hallucination. He hated Wellington and Sir John Moore, and he hated the Portuguese for co-operating with those enemies of the French Revolution. He got his ideas, as the British public did, from Hookham Frere, who was the British Agent in Spain and played the sort of rôle that Sir Ronald Storrs played in the Middle east in World War One. These literary politicians are powerless against local colour—a gyppo's nightie sets them all agog. Frere starved the British and Portuguese soldiers and spent all the money at his disposal on the worthless Spanish regulars, who did nothing but run away or sulk in the rear (except at Bailén) as did the worthless Arab lavies on whom such vast sums were spent under Lawrence. It is the same sort of love of the exotic which prefers native troops to ones own, as being more picturesque, the same sort of Romanticism which made Churchill hail Stalin as a brother, friend, and ally, allow his wife to raise a fund of millions for the Russians, and then walk right into the Booby-Trap at Yalta, where half-Christendom was sold for a bottle of Vodka. If what was happening was even obvious to a fat-head sergeant-major like me, as you can see from the satires I published in 1945, one can see there are no limits to this sort of infatuation amongst romantic literary minds in responsible positions.[27] Wellington, and history flatly contradict the late General Crozier and Lord Byron in their false estimate of Portuguese valour and the myth derived from Lord Byron and circulated after World War One, concerning the lack of courage in the Portuguese. The Spanish guerrillas did not do so badly—there Byron was right enough! I am closely related to the family of Castaños, the victor of the Bailén, so it goes somewhat against the grain to admit that he and his regulars (eulogized by Hookham Frere, as Storrs eulogized Lawrence's Arabs) ran away in nearly every other battle fought by him: and that the reverse of what Byron wrote was true at the time. But for Dupont's sudden panic at Bailén Castaños would never have become the Duke of Bailén, the Portuguese fastness.

As to Portuguese naval valour, the vast empire conquered by a country which numbered less than a million and a half inhabitants at the time, is a testimony in itself. I have sailed and worked on the Durban Whalers, with Norwegians, who are the next best sailors in the world to the Portuguese (who are the Phoenicians of the modern world). It was the Norwegians who discovered America before the Welsh Prince, Madoc founded the Mandan tribe, with their partly-Welsh vocabulary, blue eyes, and purely Welsh cradles and coracles (instead of the usual canoes used by American Indians). But I have never seen whalers or fisherman, who could equal those of the Azores, Sezimbra or Figueira de Foz, with their surf-shooting, lateen-rigged, crescent-shaped fishing-boats that put forth and return in all weathers. The fishermen of the Azores hunt blue whales, or sulphur bottoms, with hand harpoons. Of the three great sea-faring races, the Portuguese must be placed before the Phoeni-cians and the Norsemen, since, with almost the same types of vessels, they performed greater voyages, though it was Sebas-tian del Cano, on a Spanish expedition, who first circumnavi-gated the globe. Apart from the invention of the quadrant the actual rigging and sails were not much of an advance on those of the Phoenicians. Galleys were still used, in those days. Having established this, we establish Pessoa's perfect right to Pessoa's very un-Pessoa-like heroics in *Mensagem*, which can only be compared to those of Camões, Ercilla, Virgil, and Horace: or, in English, certain poems by Drayton, or Dryden's superb *Annus Mirabilis*. There is no Rhodomontade about *Mensagem*—it celebrates a reality. Pessoa was a man who superimposed a DREAM over the whole of his life as thoroughly as Don Quixote did, though, unlike Don Quixote, he never woke from his dream. Reality to him was what dreams are to us. Inside the reality that was, for him, his dream, he dreamed *Mensagem*: and as two negatives make a plus, the one dream involved in the other dream became a positive reality, historically true; and by his own standards, (and by the same double involution) so insincerely insincere—as to be utterly sincere! (At the risk of reminding you of Graves—Riding technique I refuse to delete the last sentence.) Yeats, somewhere, expresses a theory that poetry is written by the poet to compensate what he lacks. The volcanically irrepressible Landor writes with an Olympian calm: the timid and shrinking Spender[28] can be ferociously bloodthirsty and brutal; Lorca, the poet of the bullring, the horse-trade, tamers of steeds and rivers, and the knife-fighting gypsies of Spain—could neither torear, fight, ride, nor swim, but was entirely sedentary. The tiny and impotent Swinburne was all for bosoms and buttocks and falls in love with the great swashbuckling circus-amazon Ada Menken, in her Mazeppa act—with whom he could do nothing. And so on! At least half the poets of this world are the reverse of their poetry in character. The other half (here Yeats was wrong) are completely identified with their poetry, which is simply a reflection of their lives. These are generally masculine poets[.] Camões, Lope, Mistral, Sidney, Crashaw, Espronceda, St John of the Cross, Ercilla (whose poetry might be his diary) Lovelace, Herbert, Byron, and hundreds more—are identical in their lives and in their poetry. Both principles operate according as the poet writes for compensation or pleasure. Pessoa combined both these principles. He was gentle, shy, and retiring in the poetry he wrote under his own name—the best poetry he wrote. But he was fiercely aggressive, rude, cruel, and rough, in the poems he wrote under the name of *Álvaro dos Campos*. He could either be himself, or his opposite, at will.

3. The Voyages to Durban

The sea-trip, which Baudelaire made in his youth to and from Mauritius, had an incalculable effect on his work ever afterwards. We cannot imagine his work without his favourite image of a ship, and without the palms and tamarinds waving in the background. The two most intimately autobiographical of his poems "L'Albatros" and "Le Voyage," though written many years after, are memories of that voyage. The mere presence of a negress could never have evoked such imagery had he not seen and lived it, had he not possessed it, as all poets possess, forever, what they have once seen, heard, smelt or touched—to use as a foil to the mist and mud of Paris. Both the opposites in this clash of different imageries enhance their reality through the violence of the contrast between remembered sunlight and present mist. Baudelaire lived in both. Similarly Pessoa had a two fold mental habitat and was amphibious to sea and land though he remained ashore ever afterwards. I did the same trip at about the same age, like Baudelaire, as a supercargo, being the only non-professional on board. I know from my own experience what a tremendous stimulus such a voyage is, at that age, to ones poetry. And though I have since made the same trip several times by ship and by air (with magnificent panoramas of Kilimanjaro, Kenya, the Congo, atmospheric storms, Ruwenzori, the Zambezi falls, the Canary Islands, the Sahara, and God knows what else besides!)—it is from that first trip at the age of seventeen that I draw my real inspiration. The effect of the same voyage on Pessoa was even more lasting. Pessoa's mother married by proxy the Portuguese Consul at Durban, The Commandant João Miguel Rosa, whose wooing, some month's before, had so estranged[29] the jealous young Fernando. She was married in the church of São Mamede: her husband's elder brother, General Henrique Rosa, deputised as proxy for Dom João. This general was a "strange creature" and in later life he was by no means indifferent to the literary talent of his nephew-in-law. He wore the most flamboyant pair of handlebar moustaches I have ever seen—even in a photo. They were almost the size of buffalo-horns. The mad grandmother was put away in a home. Dona Madalena had embarked on twenty-five years of prosperous and happy marriage with a large new family. A week later she sailed from Lisbon to Durban, accompanied by the seven-year-old Fernando, and her brother, "Uncle Cunha," who sailed for the sole purpose of handing her over ceremoniously to the Commandant, João Miguel Rosa, in Durban—and returned as soon as he had done so. This was in 1896. He did the trip and the return-trip twice. Durban was then very much as I knew it as a child. Its rapid growth to a City began after the first World War and has not stopped ever since. Today it has about 190,000 inhabitants. Then, it had under 30,000. Nowhere in the world were there more beautiful gardens, though most of the houses had ugly corrugated iron roofs. In those days, each house reposed amidst several acres of fruit trees and flowers. Flowering trees, Jacaranda, Tulip-trees, Flame-trees, Golden Shower, Flamboyants, Kaffirboom (the most brilliant of all) and Mimosa succeed each other throughout the year (like phoenixes taking fire from each others ashes) to culminate in the gorgeous blaze of the winter-flowering Kaffirboom. As the Pessoas were neighbours of ours, on the Berea, they must have had a house and garden very much like ours. We had ten acres at the corner of Musgrave and Berea Roads. The site is now covered with sky-scraping flats and hotels. But we not only had the flowering trees I have mentioned, but about thirty different kinds of fruit—lychees, mangos, guavas, chinese guavas, pomegranates, grenadillas, avocado pears, grapes, sweet lemons, lemons, Brazil nuts, tangerines, mandarins, oranges, rose-apples, peaches, amantingulas, gulingulas, umtundulagas, coconuts, monkey apples, custard apples, wild figs, lokwats, bananas, strawberries, loganberries, and tree tomatoes, besides every sort of English and African table vegetables. The paddock for our horses was full of mango trees. A magnificent wild fig tree shadowed acres, and in it swung the nests of a singing colony of golden weaver birds who stripped our palm trees for their wicker-work nests. Here, too, would come, when the figs were ripe, emerald and sapphire starlings with orange and golden eyes: or lovies, some blue, some green, but all with flaming scar-

let wingfeathers. We had also two giant thunder trees, survivors
of the primaeval forest, and a huge tree belonging to the baobab
type, between the lowest fork of whose branches six children
could seat themselves to have tea. I never went inside the gate of
the Pessoas' garden on Ridge Road but it was probably similar
to ours. Today the architecture of the residential quarter has
been improved by copying the Cape Dutch style with white-
washed walls and tiled roofs, which in its turn was copied from
Spanish Architecture, the best for sunny climates. Durban was,
and still is, a paradise for children—especially for boys: and
Fernando Pessoa must have passed many happy days there in
spite of having to share his beloved mother with a hated step-
father. The residential quarter, the Berea, of Durban, looks over
a fine harbour. Though Durban cannot compete with the panorama of Lisbon and the Tagus, the sea is far more noble, and the
breakers steeper and bigger than on the Atlantic coast. I live
now on the westernmost point of Europe, the Promontorium
Maximum of the Romans, Cabo da Roca of the Portuguese, but
I have never seen waves roll in here like those on the coast of
Natal. The Indian and the Pacific are really one ocean so that
the waves have a far greater distance in which to gather mo-
mentum and size. It is hard to find waves that one can surf without a board in Europe. The People of Durban, as most soldiers
who went out east in the last war will remember, are almost fanatically hospitable to strangers: and the Portuguese colony
there enjoy considerable prestige and respect—partly on account of the fact that they insist on paying bills!! I have heard
both my brothers and my Father, quite independently of each
other, mention this fact in a sort of wistfully wondering way, as
if it were a strange form of eccentricity. They are doctors, and
quite used to having their doctor's bills completely ignored in
the happy-go-lucky squandering life that goes on in the town,
where everybody is reckless, generous, and spendthrift. That
Durban Docks, equally with those of Lisbon, inspired the dock
scenes in the great *Maritime Ode* I confirmed by a bit of detec-
tion[30] of which I am very proud, for the coal dust on the Lisbon
quays only shines jet black: the Durban coal dust shines with
pyrites, and twinkles like rippled water. Here is the passage that
recalls his setting out for Durban.

The mooring and unmooring of a ship—
I feel it in me as I feel my blood—
Unconsciously symbolical, and terribly
Menacing in its metaphysic significances
Which wake in me the person I was once . . .

Ah! every quay is a memory of stone!
And when the ship moves from the quay
And one notices the gap that opens
Between the quay-side and the ship-side,
There visits me a bygone anguish,
A haze of mournful sentiments
Which is tinged by, and shines in, the sun of my griefs,
Like the first window in the town to catch the morning sunbeam,
And surrounds me like the memory
Of a different, other personality,
Which none the less was mine once, in the past.

Ah who can tell? who knows
If I did not set forth, before myself,
From a quay-side; if I did not abandon
Like a vessel in the slanting rays of dawn,
Another type of port?
Who knows if, before now, before the time
Of this exterior world, as now I see it,
I have not sailed from a great quay side, full
Of a few people, from a half-awakened city,
A vast commercial city, as swelled and apoplectic
As can be found outside of Time and Space.

Yes from a Quay, in some sense quite material,
Real, and visible really as a quay,
The Absolute One Quay, whose primal model,
Unconsciously, we humans imitate,
Insensibly evoking it,
When we construct the quays in our own harbours,
Our quays of stone over authentic water,
Which are no sooner built than they announce
Themselves, quite suddenly, to be
Real-Things, Things-of-the Spirit, Entities
Of the Stone-Soul, at certain moments
When we connect with our root-sentiment,
When in the exterior world, as if a door were opened,

Without anything altering in the least,
All things are revealed in their diversity.

Ah, the Great Quay from which we sailed in Nation-ships!
Oh Grand Anterior Quay, eternal and divine!
From what port? In what waters? (And why, then, do I think it?)
Quay like all other Quays, but the Unique, the Sole!
Full, like the others, of hushed rumours before dawn,
And burgeoning at dawn into a roar of winches
With arrivals of goods-trains, beneath
The smoke of the factory-chimneys, that shadows
A floor black with glittering coal-dust, as if
A cloud were to pass over dark, twinkling ripples of water.

Essential mystery and feeling, poised
In a divine rapture of revelation
During hours the colour of silence and anguish!
There is no bridge or gangway between other quays and THE QUAY.

Quays which are blackly mirrored in still waters,
Bustle on board the ships,
The wandering instability of the souls of passengers
Of the symbolic folk who pass, and with whom naught remains,
Because whenever ships come into harbour
There always has to be some alteration
Made on board of each of them!
Continual flight! Intoxication
Of the Diverse! Eternal soul of navigators
And of their navigations! Hulls reflected
When ships are leaving harbour!
To fluctuate like the soul of life, to go
Forth like a voice, and to exist for one
Tremulous moment on the eternal waters.[31]

• • •

In a divine ecstatic revelation
During hours the colour of silence and anguish—
There is no bridge between The Quay and any other!
Quay darkly reflected in the stilled water,
There's a bustle on board of the ships,
The errant, unstable soul of the people embarked,
The symbolical people that pass, and with whom nothing endures,
Is that whenever a ship returns into harbour,

There's always some alteration that's been made to it.
Continual flights, and goings, the intoxication of Diversity!
The eternal soul of Navigators and Navigations!
Hulls slowly reflected in the water
As ships put forth from harbour!
To fluctuate like the soul of life, depart like a voice,
Live tremulous for a moment on waters eternal,
To awaken to days more direct than the days of Europe
To see strange ports on the solitude of the seas
To veer round capes into vast panoramas
By numberless, wondering hillsides . . .

Ah the distant shores and the quays seen far away!
Then the nearing shore, and the quays seen near at hand!
The mystery of each departure and arrival
The sad incomprehensibility and unstableness
Of this impossible universe
At each maritime hour that is felt in the skin as it passes!
The absurd sop that our spirits give forth
Over the different expanses of sea with their far-off isles,
Over the distant islands with coasts left behind,
Over the clear growth of harbours, with their houses and people
      getting larger,
To the ship that is surely approaching . . .

This memory of a different other person who was so mysteriously himself was a memory of the wrench of parting from the "village square" and all he had held dear, all things with which he had hitherto identified himself, the wrench of the knowledge that his mother would from now cease to belong to him. In parting from the quay at Lisbon he left the other self—which he used to be—behind him. As Dr Gaspar Simões says, "This was the point of departure for a metaphysical divagation and also for a sadistic vision of a savage piratical butchery in which children are sacrificed before the horrified eyes of their parents (a terrible torture was his in that hour of parting, under the eyes of his mother, who was, for him, at the same time, purely, his torturer.)" This *Maritime Ode* would never have existed had it not been for this departure, this terrible decisive departure from a quay which the very poet himself, in this strange composition, associates with an 'ancestral quay' from which he once departed, in some other existence, before he became himself."

Now we come to one of the strangest[32] things in the whole of Pessoa's life. His ten years in Durban, where he learnt the English language so well, that he had no trace of a colonial accent, and where he stripped most of the school-prizes from his British colonial competitors, left absolutely no trace on his writings except that he corresponded for twenty years with his friend, Mr. Ormond. It is only the quays and the dockside of that "City of the towering ships," and the coastline of the Indian Ocean that made an impression on him: and what an impression!

The most famous passage in the whole of Portuguese literature is that astounding apparition of Adamastor, the spirit of the "Cape of Storms," as it used to be called, or "the Cape of Good Hope" as it had to be rechristened, for fear of discouraging the sailors. The Cape coast with its craggy headlands was remembered by Sir Walter Raleigh as by far the most memorable sight he encountered on his voyage round the world. The conquest of the Cape was quite as much of a spiritual and moral victory as a geographical one. It was the first practical realisation of the fact that one could not fall off the edge of the Earth. Armand Guibert, in his delightful book on Prince Henry the Navigator who was half English on his mother's side, points out that he is rather the last of the mediaeval than one of the first of the Renaissance figures. The purpose behind all his scientific and astronomical research, was the purpose of the missionary and the crusader. The trade motive and the rivalry with Venice was secondary to this main purpose.

To a Portuguese, the Cape has the very deepest significance. It is a religious, historical, racial and literary symbol. In a country where poetry is given such importance (as in Portugal) where almost every educated person writes verse, it naturally has a vast importance as having inspired the greatest passage in the national literature. To the average Portuguese, the importance of Camões is far greater than that of Vasco da Gama, though they lie side by side in their magnificent tombs in the Church of the Jeronymos, with Camões' faithful black slave buried at his feet. The birthday of Camões is a public holiday second only to Christmas and Easter in a Catholic country: but no public holiday celebrates any of the great navigators or empire builders. Raleigh, Melville, Camões, and who ever else amongst marine writers have seen the Cape, have been inspired by it into the most grandiose language. The mountainous Cape rollers in themselves are awe-inspiring enough with the eternal cruising backwards and forwards of the huge, archangelic albatrosses and mollymawks, the black cape-hens, cape pigeons, and sinister skuas & petrels. We are reminded of Baudelaire and Coleridge and Melville in their finest moments. As a literary symbol the Cape cast a far greater spell over Pessoa than its mere presence or view could have done.[33]

But we have seen that he could be utterly indifferent to landscape when it had no literary associations, for the extraordinary beauty of Natal left him completely cold. Yet the bleak[34] and stormy desolation of the towering peninsula having struck his imagination first of all through the reading of poetry, must have haunted his memory as did the shipping in the Tagus-mouth: and it is not difficult to see in the "Mostrengo" the ghastly spirit that lives at the farthest ends of the Ocean, the son and heir of Adamastor himself.

• • •

> The Monstrous thing that at the verge
> Of ocean lives, rose from the surge
> On a wild night. He sped three times
> Around the ship his flight to urge
> Three times he howled Who's this who climbs
> Upon my roof who comes to brave
> The terrors of my yawning cave
> In which the darkness is so fecund.
> The trembling steersman answer gave
> It's King Don John the Second

• • •

> Three times he let his hands go slack
> Three times again he put them back
> Three times he trembled then he said
> Here at this helm I'm more than one

I am a race that loves your sea
And if there's anything I dread
More than a monstrous thing, It's he
Upon whose service I am beckoned
At the world's end, unmapped, unreckoned,
Who lords my will to and is to me
My King Don John the second.[35]

Notes

1. Works and Days

1. Bloom, *The Western Canon*, 463-92; and Steiner, "Foursome," 76-80.

2. Examples of Benoit van Innis's drawings appear in the *New Yorker*, June 21, 1993, p. 62; April 3, 1995, p. 44; and June 26 & July 3, 1995, p. 66.

3. Adolfo Casais Monteiro, *A poesia de Fernando Pessoa*, 232-33. My translation.

4. Quoted in Lisboa and Taylor, *A Centenary Pessoa*, 133-34.

5. Lopes, *II: Pessoa por conhecer*, 379. My translation.

6. Roditi, "Fernando Pessoa," 380.

7. Vidigal, "Note," iii-v.

8. *Alberto de Lacerda*, 61; Roditi, "The Several Names of Fernando Pessoa," 40-44; and Burnshaw, *The Poem Itself*, 198-201.

9. Hamburger, *The Truth of Poetry*, 138-47.

10. Merton, *A Vow of Conversation*, 56-57.

11. Wain, "Thinking About Mr. Person," 75.

12. Adolfo Casais Monteiro, *A poesia de Fernando Pessoa*, 230, 246. My translation.

13. Quoted in George Monteiro, "Jorge de Sena/Edith Sitwell: Correspondence," 11.

14. Quoted in George Monteiro, "Jorge de Sena/Edith Sitwell: Correspondence," 12.

15. Quoted in George Monteiro, "Jorge de Sena/Edith Sitwell: Correspondence," 17.

16. Sena, "Resposta a três perguntas," 2:175. My translation.

17. When Sena approached Roy Campbell for help with the difficulties he found in the English of Pessoa's sonnets, he got a different reaction. The South African admired Pessoa's Portuguese poems, but he was hostile to the "English" poems and discouraged any attempt to translate them into Portuguese. Campbell insisted that he too was unable to understand many of the passages that perplexed Sena and Adolfo Casais Monteiro, Sena's collaborator in the translation project. Sena's explanation for Campbell's hostility was: "Maybe he was merely hostile to language that Pessoa had taken to incredible heights of literary-syntactical complication, though it was not entirely the case that he hated the poetry's complex ambiguity. He was really reacting against literary

137

expression that comes across as much too labored, that does not always succeed" ("Resposta a três perguntas," 174). My translation.

18. Leckey, "Borges for Breakfast," 32.

19. Bloom, *The Western Canon*, 463.

20. Bloom, *The Western Canon*, 490-91.

21. Bloom, *The Western Canon*, 492.

22. White, "The Hearts of Men," 96. White's title echoes the words of "The Shadow" (the crime-fighting hero of a weekly drama over American radio in the 1930s and 1940s), who claimed to know "what evil lurks in the hearts of men."

23. John Hollander, "Quadrophenia," 36.

24. Quoted in *Poems of Fernando Pessoa*, back of dust jacket.

25. Quoted in *Poems of Fernando Pessoa*, back of dust jacket.

26. Quoted in *Poems of Fernando Pessoa*, back of dust jacket.

27. Quoted from the London *Sunday Times* on the back cover of *Selected Poems*, trans. Jonathan Griffin, 2d ed.

28. Bloom, *The Western Canon*, 548-67.

29. Brodsky, "How to Read a Book,"29, and Schwerner, "Old Dog Sermon," 87.

30. Shange, *Spell #7*, 34.

2. Old School Loyalties

1. Campbell, "A South African Poet in Portugal," in *Collected Works IV*, 434.

2. Deutsch, "American and British Verse," 117.

3. Rodway, "Foreword," *Poetry of the 1930s*, ix.

4. Review of Roy Campbell's *Mithraic Emblems*, 26.

5. "Rum Tum Tum on a Broken Drum," 52, 54.

6. Smith, Review, 140.

7. Paton, Review of Rowland Smith's *Lyric and Polemic*, 120.

8. Campbell, "Translator's Note," vi.

9. See H[arold] V. L[ivermore], Review of Roy Campbell's translation of *O primo Basílio*, 48-49.

10. Campbell, "Olive Schreiner," 1. The manuscript continues: "The cast-iron leg of this desk was broken one day, and the desk was used for fire-wood under the boiler for the laundry."

11. Alexander, *Roy Campbell*, 74. Some eighty years earlier Herman Melville's imagination had also been fired by Mickle's translation, first in *White-Jacket* (1850) and then in *Moby-Dick* (1851).

12. Roy Campbell to Edith Sitwell, n.d., Edith Sitwell Collection, Harry Ransom Humanities Research Center, Univ. of Texas at Austin.

13. Campbell, *Adamastor*, 107. The ways in which southern African poets have used and transvalued "Adamastor" as both a European and an African symbol are discussed in my book *The Presence of Camões: Influences on the Literature of England, America, and Southern Africa* (Lexington: Univ. Press of Kentucky, 1996), 120-31.

14. Campbell, "Luís de Camões," in *Talking Bronco*, 11. The volume in-

cludes a second poetic tribute to Camões, "Imitation (and Endorsement) of the Famous Sonnet of Bocage which he Wrote on Active Service Out East" (52).

15. Campbell, *Portugal*, 142.
16. Campbell, *Light on a Dark Horse*, 174.
17. Campbell, "Olive Schreiner."
18. Roy Campbell, "Roy Campbell on J. Paço d'Arcos," in *Nostalgia: A Collection of Poems*, trans. Roy Campbell (London: Sylvan Press, 1960), 5. Paço d'Arcos's title is *Poemas imperfeitos*.
19. Alexander, *Roy Campbell*, 227.
20. Alexander, *Roy Campbell*, 236.
21. Campbell, *Portugal*, 156.
22. Campbell's translations are preceded only by Charles David Ley's of the poem beginning "O céu, azul de luz quieta" in *Presença* in 1938; Leonard S. Downes's of "Mar português" ("Mare nostrum") and "Epitáfio de Bartolomeu Dias" ("Epitaph for Batholomeu Dias") in *Portuguese Poems and Translations*, 43-44; and Roditi's of a few lines by Álvaro de Campos in "The Several Names of Fernando Pessoa," 43-44.

23. Bell, *Oxford Book of Portuguese Verse*, 2d ed. Campbell seems to have worked often from this text. Of the eleven Portuguese poets Campbell translated—Mendinho, Pero Meogo, Airas Nunez, Gil Vicente, Luís de Camões, Bocage, Antero de Quental, Fernando Pessoa, José Régio, Carlos Queiroz, and Joaquim Paço d'Arcos—seven are represented in the *Oxford Book*. Of Campbell's published translations from Portuguese poetry, the originals of the following appear in the *Oxford Book:* Mendinho's "Cantiga de Romaria," Pero Meogo's "Cantiga de Amigo" ("Tal vai o meu amigo") and "Cossante," Airas Nunez's "Bailada," Gil Vicente's "Romance," Camões's "Jacob e Raquel" and "Alma minha gentil," and Bocage's "Contrição."

Campbell's finished translations from Portuguese poetry are gathered in his *Collected Works II*, (1985), 303-31, 439-77. Manuscript versions survive of two other poems published in the *Oxford Book:* Pessoa's "Mar português" (complete) and "O Mostrengo" (two stanzas)—both from *Mensagem*. Campbell's version of stanzas 1 and 3 of "O Mostrengo" appear at the end of his manuscript on Pessoa (see Appendix). The most nearly finished copy of "Mar português" is published here for the first time:

> How much of your salt waves, O sea,
> The tears of Portugal must be!
> How many mothers wept their loss
> And sons have vainly prayed—to cross
> Your deeps. How many maids have tarried,
> To make you ours, unmarried.
>
> Was it worth while? Yes worth it all,
> If the soul is not mean or small.
> He who would pass Cape Bojador
> Must round the Cape of Grief before.
> God gave the sea its dangers, true.
> But heaven is mirrored in its blue.

24. Vidigal, "Note," v.

25. João Gaspar Simões tells the story in *Fernando Pessoa*, 9-10. Simões's book, which has not appeared in English, was published twice before 1983: as *Fernando Pessoa: Escorço interpretativo da sua vida e obra* and as "Uma explicação da vida e da obra de Fernando Pessoa." On page 11 of "Uma explicação" he offers a less detailed account of how he came to write this study of Pessoa.

26. Campbell, "A South African Poet in Portugal," in *Collected Works IV*, 434.

27. Campbell, *Portugal*, 156, 158-60.

28. Ms. (undated), Harry Ransom Humanities Research Center, Univ. of Texas at Austin.

29. Ms. (undated), Harry Ransom Humanities Research Center, Univ. of Texas at Austin.

30. Alexander, *Roy Campbell*, 233.

31. Perhaps some light is shed on Campbell's repudiation of Lawrence by William Plomer, Campbell's friend and fellow editor of the journal *Voorslag*, who in 1930 writes: "I hope you won't mind my saying that I hope you're not going to develop the mania that Roy [Campbell] & Wyndham Lewis have about homosexuality. I am always extremely suspicious of such an attitude, which usually comes from frustration. I have reason to know that both Roy & Lewis have experimented with their own sex, & I cannot but feel that their present violence is quite pathological. They both protest too much. . . . The artist who makes a song about his maleness (or his femaleness, as the case may be) is lacking in honesty, for it is a platitude that every artist is in a sense bi-sexual" (quoted in Alexander, *William Plomer*, 170).

32. Campbell, "A South African Poet in Portugal," *Collected Works IV*, 434.

33. Sena, "Resposta a três perguntas," 2:174.

34. Roy Campbell to Hubert D. Jennings, quoted by Jack Cope in his editorial headnote to Jennings's "The Many Faces of Pessoa," 51.

3. Poet and Antipoet

1. Edmund White and Edouard Roditi, "Conversation on an Island in the Seine," 150.

2. His titles include *Poems for F* (1935), *Poems, 1928-1948* (1949), *Emperor of Midnight* (1974), *Oscar Wilde: A Critical Guidebook* (1947; rev. 1986), *Joachim Karsch* (1960), *Magellan of the Pacific* (1972), *The Disorderly Poet* (1975), *The Delights of Turkey: Twenty Tales* (1977), *Meetings With Conrad* (1977), and *De l'Homosexualité* (1962).

3. Thomas Epstein, "On the Usefulness of Dinosaurs or *le cas* Edouard Roditi," 135.

4. "Sieben Gedichte," 401-10.

5. Roditi, "The Several Names of Fernando Pessoa," 40-44. The pieces published in Portugal are "Fernando Pessoa, forasteiro entre os poetas ingleses," and "A máscara inglesa de Fernando Pessoa."

6. Roditi, "Autopsychoanalysis," 27.

7. Pessoa, *Self-Analysis and Thirty Other Poems*, 17.

8. Roditi, "The Warning," 26.

9. *Poemas ingleses*, 1:84.

10. Pessoa, "English Poems," 385-91.

11. *Poemas ingleses*, 1:75.

12. Roditi, "The Several Names of Fernando Pessoa," 41.

13. Merton, *The Hidden Ground of Love*, 192.

14. Merton, *The School of Charity*, 227. The context of Merton's remark is worth noting. At the time he was reading Latin American poets. "There is a kind of religious night, an anguish very deep but simple with Vallejo—a Peruvian Indian. . . . what one finds in him is simply a very pure awareness of God, very simple and without grand articulation. And no fuss or bother. It is these very people to whom we can listen with profit. Vallejo is certainly, in a very obscure way, a prophet of our time and our hemisphere. A witness of our misery and confusion. He is the Incas' version of Baudelaire, and so simple. I have also started to read a Portuguese of the same type, Pessoa. He also describes the dark night" (227).

15. Merton, *Zen and the Birds of Appetite*, 119.

16. Merton, *Zen and the Birds of Appetite*, 129.

17. Merton, *The Hidden Ground of Love*, 561. Of his hermitage at the Abbey of Gethsemani, Trappist, Kentucky, he wrote: "Up here in the woods is seen the New Testament: that is to say, the wind comes through the trees and you breathe it" ("Day of a Stranger," 214).

18. Merton, *The Hidden Ground of Love*, 192. At this time Merton asked Sister M. Emmanuel de Souza e Silva, his Brazilian translator, to find him a copy of Pessoa in Portuguese. "There is one thing perhaps someone in Rio could get for me: I have run across the Portuguese poet Fernando Pessoa, who also wrote under three or four different pen names. Octavio Paz has translated selections from him into Spanish. I would like very much to have him in Portuguese, and I think his works are obtainable in Rio, for one edition was published there. Could you give someone the good idea of finding them for me?" (191). Although Merton in the end published translations of twelve of Caeiro's poems, as did Paz, in the main their choices were different, overlapping in only three instances.

19. Merton, *The Courage for Truth*, 192.

20. Merton, *The Courage for Truth*, 147. Emphasis added.

21. Merton, *A Vow of Conversation*, 56-57.

22. Merton, *The Hidden Ground of Love*, 460.

23. Pessoa, "Twelve Poems," 299. The poems appear on pp. 299-307. They are reprinted as "From the Portuguese of Fernando Pessoa: Twelve Poems from *The Keeper of the Flocks*," in *The Collected Poems of Thomas Merton*, 987-96. Merton's "Translator's Note" appears in *The Literary Essays of Thomas Merton*, where the editor states erroneously that it is being published for the first time, having been "found among Merton's unpublished manuscripts following his death" (309; see also x).

24. Merton, *The Hidden Ground of Love*, 461.

25. Merton, "Day of a Stranger," 212.

26. "I have a terrible cold," in *Poems of Fernando Pessoa*, 97; *Poemas de Álvaro de Campos*, 307-8.

27. Merton, *Zen and the Birds of Appetite*, 140.
28. Pessoa, "Twelve Poems," 306-7.
29. Pessoa, "Twelve Poems," 302. On Merton's interest in the Zen-like qualities of the poetry of Pessoa-Caeiro and a tracing of both subsequent and independently generated interest in a "Zen" Pessoa, see Almeida, "Sobre a mundividência Zen."
30. Merton, *A Vow of Conversation*, 160.
31. Merton, *A Vow of Conversation*, 138.
32. Mécia de Sena, *Eduardo Lourenço/Jorge de Sena correspondência*, 71. My translation.
33. Hamburger, *The Truth of Poetry*, 141.
34. Hamburger, *The Truth of Poetry*, 141.
35. Quoted in Shannon, *Thomas Merton's Dark Path*, 58.
36. Quoted in Shannon, *Thomas Merton's Dark Path*, 58.
37. Pessoa, "Salutation to Walt Whitman," in *Poems of Fernando Pessoa*, 73.
38. Merton, *Cables to the Ace*, 395.
39. Merton, *Cables to the Ace*, 430.
40. Pessoa, *Self-Analysis and Thirty Other Poems*, 55.
41. Quoted in Shannon, *Thomas Merton's Dark Path*, 70.

4. Dominoes

1. *Poetic Translation*, 41.
2. Honig, "Fernando Pessoa: A Translator's View," 137.
3. Honig, "Introduction," 6.
4. Honig, "Translator's Note," 103.
5. Pessoa, "Twelve Poems," 299. Honig dedicated his lyric sequence *Gifts of Light* "To the life, work, and spirit of Thomas Merton."
6. Honig, "Preface," x.
7. Honig, "Preface," x.
8. Shapiro, "On First Looking into Honig's Pessoa," back cover.
9. Octavio Paz, "Introduction," *Selected Poems by Fernando Pessoa*, 1-21. The essay is available in Paz, *Cuadrivio*, 93-113.
10. Matos, "Edwin Honig and Jean Longland," 154-55.
11. Honig, "Introduction," 6.
12. Honig, *Interrupted Praise*, 54.
13. Pessoa, *Always Astonished*, ii.
14. Honig, *Interrupted Praise*, 33-37.
15. Pessoa, *Always Astonished*, ii.
16. Matos, "Edwin Honig and Jean Longland," 153.
17. Sena, *A literatura inglêsa*, 437.
18. Honig, "Translator's View," 135-36.
19. Honig, "Translator's View," 137.
20. Honig, *Dark Conceit*, 80, 133, and 161.
21. Honig, "Translator's View," 137. The slightly different version quoted comes from Honig, "Introduction: Some Words in the Entryway," viii-ix. The poem is also reprinted in Honig, *The Imminence of Love*, 49.

22. Roditi, "The Several Names of Fernando Pessoa," 40. Roditi also seems to be the first one to employ the word "feign" in connection with Pessoa's notions about poetry. "All poetry, in Pessoa's eyes, was indeed simulation, and all poets, according to his faith," concludes Roditi, "are most sincere when least sincere, most truthful when they feign" (44). In this he anticipates at least three of Pessoa's translators, namely Ernesto Guerra Da Cal (Burnshaw, *The Poem Itself*, 198), Michael Hamburger (*The Truth of Poetry*, 142), and Jean Longland (Pessoa, "Translations," 280), all of whom use the term in their English versions of "Autopsicografia."

23. "Tabacaria," *Poemas de Álvaro de Campos*, 199. My translation.

24. *Poemas de Álvaro de Campos*, 252. My translation.

25. Paz, *Cuadrivio*, 93. My translation.

26. Pessoa, *35 Sonnets*, in *Poemas ingleses*, 1:70. This notion of the writer's emotional sleight-of-hand is presented in an aesthetically more pleasing fashion in "Autopscografia," Pessoa's perhaps not so tongue-in-cheek poem of 1932, quoted here in the Honig-Brown translation (*Poems of Fernando Pessoa*, 149):

> The poet is a faker. He
> Fakes it so completely,
> He even fakes he's suffering
> The pain he's really feeling.
>
> And they who read his writing
> Fully feel while reading
> Not that pain of his that's double,
> But theirs, completely fictional.
>
> So on its tracks goes round and round,
> To entertain the reason,
> That wound-up little train
> We call the heart of man.

27. *Orpheu* 1, plate between pp. xxiv and xxv. My translation.

28. Pessoa, *Ultimatum*, 114. My translation. In notes set down three or four years earlier to announce the beginning of a "Golden Age of Portuguese literature," Pessoa had cautioned his Portuguese readers not to be "confounded with things like the 'Celtic Revival' or any Yeats fairy-nonsense" (*Páginas íntimas*, 119).

29. Álvaro de Campos, "Ambiente," in Pessoa, *Textos de crítica e de intervenção*, 264. My translation.

30. Yeats, *The Player Queen*, quoted in Ellmann, *Yeats: The Man and the Masks*, 176.

31. Honig, "An Open Reply to August Willemsen," 52.

5. City Lights

1. Ferreira e Sousa, "Lawrence Ferlinghetti," 7.

2. Quoted in Silesky, *Ferlinghetti*, 228.

3. Ferlinghetti, *Love in the Days of Rage*, dedication page. Further quotations from this source are documented by page numbers in the text.

4. As early as 1978 Ferlinghetti identifies himself with his maternal grandfather by identifying the editor of the fourth issue of *City Lights Journal* as "Mendes Monsanto"; and in 1983 he assigns his preface to "Leaves of Life: Fifty Drawings from the Model," a selection of his own work, to Mendes Monsanto (Silesky, *Ferlinghetti*, 212-13).

5. Pessoa, "Le banquier anarchiste," translated by A. Coyné, in *Exils* 819 (Spring/Summer 1978); listed in Blanco, *Fernando Pessoa: esboço de uma bibliografia*, 465. Joaquim Vital's version—*Le banquier anarchiste* (Paris: Littérature/Editions de la Différence, 1988)—appeared in the year Ferlinghetti published *Love in the Days of Rage*.

6. Ferlinghetti, "Director of Alienation," quoted in Silesky, *Ferlinghetti*, 195.

7. Pessoa, "The Anarchist Banker: A Fiction," 82. Further quotations from this source are documented by page numbers in the text.

8. Ferlinghetti, "I Am Waiting," in *A Coney Island of the Mind*, 49.

9. K., "Fernando Pessoa," in Pessoa, *O banqueiro anarquista*, 9. Quotations from this essay are given in my translation.

10. K., "Fernando Pessoa," 11-12.

11. K., "Fernando Pessoa," 12.

12. An exception is Ellen Sapega's "On Logical Contradictions and Contradictory Logic: Fernando Pessoa's *O banqueiro anarquista*," *Luso-Brazilian Review 26* (Summer l989), 111-18.

13. Lopes, *Pessoa inédito*, 379. My translation.

14. Silesky, *Ferlinghetti*, 228.

15. Silesky, *Ferlinghetti*, 229.

16. Silesky, *Ferlinghetti*, 135.

17. Adolfo Casais Monteiro, *A poesia de Fernando Pessoa*, 230. My translation.

18. Adolfo Casais Monteiro, *A poesia de Fernando Pessoa*, 243.

19. Adolfo Casais Monteiro, *A poesia de Fernando Pessoa*, 246. My translation.

6. Barbaric Complaint

1. Perlman, Folsom, and Campion, *Walt Whitman: The Measure of His Song*, x.

2. "Allen Ginsberg on Walt Whitman," in *Walt Whitman: The Measure of His Song*, 231.

3. "Ginsberg on Walt Whitman," 231.

4. "Ginsberg on Walt Whitman," 231.

5. Folsom, "Talking Back to Walt Whitman: An Introduction," in *Walt Whitman: The Measure of His Song*, xxxx-xxxxi.

6. "Salutations to Fernando Pessoa" appears in *Bombay Gin*, n.s., 1 (Summer 1989), 94-95; *Threepenny Review* 15 (Spring 1994), 5; Ginsberg, *Cosmopolitan Greetings*, 34-35; and *The Best American Poetry*, 1995, ed. Richard Howard (New York: Simon and Schuster, 1995), 69-70.

7. Quoted in "Encerrou na Gulbenkian a Babel da Ilha Pessoana," *Europeu* (Dec. 8, 1988); reprinted in Tamen, *Um século de Pessoa*, 390-91. Honig's comment appears on p. 391.

8. *Poems of Fernando Pessoa*, 72-78.
9. *Poems of Fernando Pessoa*, 72-73.
10. *Poems of Fernando Pessoa*, 73.
11. *Cosmopolitan Greetings*, 34-35.
12. *Poems of Fernando Pessoa*, 3.
13. Pessoa, "Twelve Poems," 299-307.
14. Ginsberg, "A Supermarket in California," in *Collected Poems, 1947-1980*, 136.
15. Ginsberg, *Collected Poems, 1947-1980*, 760-61.
16. *Poems of Fernando Pessoa*, 72.
17. Ginsberg, *White Shroud: Poems, 1980-1985*, 58.

7. Blue Tiles

1. Greg Johnson, *Joyce Carol Oates*, 84.
2. Oates, *"The Poisoned Kiss" and Other Stories from the Portuguese*, 188 (subsequent page numbers appear parenthetically in the text below).
3. "The Letter," *Literary Review* 17 (Fall 1973), 1, 2, 86.
4. Fernandes, "Letters to Fernandes from a Young American Poet," *Chelsea* 30/31 (June 1972), 4, 51-58.
5. *Chelsea* 30/31 (June 1972), 204, 201.
6. Oates, "Two Young Men," *Aspen Leaves* 2 (1974), 89, 95.
7. "The Editor's Notebook," *Southwest Review* 56 (Autumn 1971), 372.
8. "Contributors," *Yale Review* 63 (Spring 1974), xvii.
9. Schumacher, "Joyce Carol Oates," 139-40.
10. Oates, "Pseudonymous Selves," 396-97.
11. Oates, *(Woman) Writer*, xiii.
12. References to "azulejos" are common enough in Portuguese poetry. In "Para além doutro oceano de C[oelho] Pacheco" ["Beyond that Further Ocean of C. Pacheco"], for example, Pessoa himself refers to the "blue tiles coloring the walls" of "a hall noble in shadows" (*Obra poética*, 430); my translation.
13. Elsewhere Oates does refer to Borges. For example, in "Does the Writer Exist?" (1984) she quotes almost the whole of "Borges and I" (49); in "Literature as Pleasure, Pleasure as Literature" (1987) she quotes Borges—"I have always come to life after coming to books"—as an epigraph ((*Woman) Writer*, 53); and in the novel *Wonderland* (1971) she quotes the final sentences of "Avatars of the Tortoise," also as an epigraph: "We . . . have dreamt the world. We have dreamt it as firm, mysterious, visible, ubiquitous in space and durable in time; but in its architecture we have allowed tenuous and eternal crevices of unreason which tell us it is false" (11).
14. Quoted in Alfredo Margarido, Introduction to Fernando Pessoa, *Santo António, São João, São Pedro* (Lisbon: A Regra do Jogo, 1986), 81, n. 25. My translation.
15. See Sena, *Fernando Pessoa & Ca Heterónima*, 2:73-79, 228-29.
16. Oates, "Does the Writer Exist?" 50.

8. Durban Echoes

1. The three poems from Pessoa's *Mensagem* are "The Blighter," "The Ascent of Vasco da Gama," and "The Portuguese Sea." The other two poems by Pessoa are "If, After I Die" (by Alberto Caeiro) and "Azure, or Green, or Purple," the latter written by "Fernando Pessoa" on June 9, 1935, six months after the publication of *Mensagem*.

2. Gray, *Penguin Book of Southern African Verse*, xix.

3. Gray, *Southern African Literature*, 24.

4. Gray, *Southern African Literature*, 15, 27.

5. Gray, *Southern African Literature*, 27.

6. Gray, *Southern African Literature*, 27-28.

7. Gray, *Southern African Literature*, 17.

8. Campbell, "Rounding the Cape," in *Selected Poetry*, 16-17.

9. Alexander, *Roy Campbell*, 74.

10. The designation is Jack Cope's ("Foreword" to Eglington, *Under the Horizon*, x; subsequent page numbers appear parenthetically in text below).

11. Eglington announced a collection of translations from the poetry of Fernando Pessoa to be published in 1967. He even went so far as to list it in his curriculum vitae as having been done, but only "The Blighter" survives.

12. When "Homage to Fernando Pessoa" was first published in *Contrast 16*, these lines served as the epigraph to three numbered poems—"Horizon," "Bartholomew Diaz," and "Fever"—identified as part of Eglington's "cycle of poems," as well as "Lourenço Marques," described as a poem "closely related" to the cycle ("Notes," 94).

13. This translation is given in *Under the Horizon* (98), but it is not identified as being Eglington's.

14. This translation is not identified as Eglington's (98). When the poem was first published in "Homage to Fernando Pessoa," *Contrast 16*, it appeared without the epigraph.

15. This translation is not identified as Eglington's (98).

16. Pessoa, "Portuguese Sea," in *Self-Analysis and Thirty Other Poems*, 21. The original reads: "Quem quere passar além do Bojador / Tem que passar além da dor. / Deus ao mar o perigo e o abysmo deu, / Mas nelle é que espelhou o céu" (*Obra poética*, 82).

17. "Horizon," in *Poems of Fernando Pessoa*, 169.

18. *Poems of Fernando Pessoa*, 170.

19. Hubert D. Jennings, the South African student of Pessoa's work, describes Eglington's practice in "Homage to Fernando Pessoa": "It is remarkable how he intertwines the themes and always adds something of his own. *Horizon* carries the spirit but nothing of the wording of the original, but phrases from *Horizonte* are bracketed on to a literal translation of *Dias* with tremendous effect; and *Fever*, perhaps the most remarkable of the three, launches not only into new voyages undreamed of by Diogo Cão, but also into seas of modern spiritual uncertainty which would also have been incomprehensible to him" (quoted in Eglington, *Under the Horizon*, xi-xii).

20. Jennings, "Eglington," 87. For an interpretation of Pessoa's forward-looking intentions in *Mensagem*, see Almeida's *Mensagem*.

21. Martin Seymour-Smith, *The New Guide to Modern World Literature*, 3d ed. rev. (New York: Peter Bedrick, 1985), 1026.

22. "Notes," *Contrast 16*, 94.

23. Pessoa's original, in Portuguese, appears in *Páginas íntimas*, 27-28.

24. For a Portuguese translation of Eglington's "Homage to Fernando Pessoa," see Eugénio Lisboa, "'Homenagem a Fernando Pessoa.'"

9. Looking for Mr. Person

1. Hamburger, *A Mug's Game*, 270.

2. Hamburger, *The Truth of Poetry*, 138.

3. Hamburger, *The Truth of Poetry*, 147.

4. Hamburger, *Testimonies*, 243.

5. Hamburger, *Testimonies*, 84.

6. Hamburger, *The Truth of Poetry*, 138.

7. Hamburger, "Author's Note," in *Collected Poems, 1941-1983*, 17.

8. Hamburger, *Collected Poems*, 276-77.

9. Pessoa, *Selected Poems*, trans. Peter Rickard, 89, 91.

10. Pessoa, *Sixty Portuguese Poems*, 103, 105. Campos's insomnia is studied by José Blanco, "Álvaro de Campos Insone," 573-86.

11. Wain, "Thinking About Mr. Person," *New Lugano Review*, 73.

12. Wain, "Glare and Shadow," 328.

13. Wain, "A Salute to the Makers," 53.

14. Wain, "Visiting an Old Poet," in *Poems, 1949-1979*, 9.

15. Wain, *The Free Zone Stops Here*, vii.

16. Harvey, "Fernando Pessoa," 16.

17. Álvaro de Campos's five poems are "The ancients invoked the Muses" ("Os antigos invocaram as Musas"), "Unfurling before an imaginary crowd of starred heavens" ("Desfraldando ao conjunto fictício dos ceus estrelados"), "I would love to love loving" ("Gostava de gostar de gostar"), "Wherever I am and go, wherever I am not, and don't go—" ("Ah, onde estou ou onde passo, ou onde não estou nem passo"), and "Tripe à la mode de Caen" ("Dobrada à moda do Porto"). Alberto Caeiro's nine poems are "The Tagus is more beautiful than the river that runs through my village" ("O Tejo é mais belo que o rio que corre pela minha aldeia"), "I've never understood how you could find a sunset sad" ("Nunca sei como é que se pode achar um poente triste"), "When spring returns" ("Quando tornar a vir a Primavera"), "Ah, so you want a better light" ("Ah, querem uma lua melhor que a do sol!"), "When the grass grows over my tomb" ("Quando a erva crescer em cima da minha sepultura"), "It isn't enough just opening the window" ("Não basta abrir a janela"), "This is, perhaps, the last day of my life" ("É talvez o último dia da minha vida"), "Sometimes, on days of perfect and exact light" ("Às vezes, em dias de luz perfeita e exata"), and "Lightly, lightly, very lightly" ("Leve, leve, muito leve"). And Ricardo Reis's six poems are "You are alone. You know that. Be quiet, and pretend" ("Estás só. Ninguém o sabe. Cala e finge"), "It is not you, Christ, whom I hate or do not love" ("Não a ti, Cristo, odeio ou te não quero"), "Innumerable beings live in us" ("Vivem em nós inúmeros"), "I await, with equanimity, the unknown"

("Aguardo, equânime, o que não conheço"), and "I prefer roses, my love, to my country" ("Prefiro rosas, meu amor, à pátria").

18. Harvey, *No Diamonds, No Hat, No Honey,* 42. Subsequent page numbers appear parenthetically in the text.

19. Recall Reis's lines: "Nothing, Lídia, do we owe / To Fate, save experiencing it" ("Nada, Lídia, devemos / Ao fado, senão tê-lo") (Pessoa, *Obra poética,* 283). My translation.

20. "Mandive House" (revised version) enclosed in a letter from Dennis Silk to the author (May 31, 1996). An earlier version appears in Brown, Epstein, and Gould, *A Glass of Green Tea—With Honig,* 175.

21. Silk, *The Punished Land,* 33.

Appendix

1. Campbell had originally entitled his first chapter "An Elusive Character."

2. Campbell crossed out "loyal affection to his dying day."

3. "Vida e Obra de Fernando Pessoa" Livraria Bertrand [Campbell's note].

4. Campbell crossed out "he can only say that the work of a poet is before anything else the work of a man: and that a man of genius is only a genius in so far as he is a man."

5. Campbell crossed out "his intimates."

6. Campbell crossed out "claims of those."

7. Contemporary Academic critics similarly misplaced their interest in the "Rowley Poems" of Chatterton. They were only interested in them as the poems of Rowley and had no time for them as the very remarkable work of the genius, Chatterton. When the heteronym was exposed all academic interest faded [Campbell's note].

8. Campbell crossed out "care."

9. In *Talking Bronco,* Campbell defines "Bint" as an Arabic word for "woman" (91). Lawrence's *The Mint: A Day-book of the RAF Depot between August and December 1922 with later Notes by 35087 A/C Ross* was first published in 1955.

10. Campbell crossed out "lusts."

11. Campbell crossed out "platonically."

12. Campbell crossed out "one inamorata."

13. Campbell crossed out "sodomite."

14. Except, imaginatively, in a long passage in his Ode Maritima [Campbell's note].

15. Campbell crossed out "gloating."

16. Campbell crossed out "romantic."

17. Campbell crossed out "more or less harmless."

18. Campbell crossed out "Though a Paracelsus or a Cagliostro at least half of him was genuine."

19. Campbell crossed out "mission."

20. Campbell crossed out "Leftwing."

21. Campbell crossed out "of the present retrogressive descent known as progress, which is really a chute to the abyss."

22. Campbell crossed out "which demolishes itself as Einstein supersedes Newton, as."

23. Campbell crossed out "demolishes."

24. Campbell crossed out "demolished."

25. Campbell crossed out "chilly."

26. Campbell crossed out "A nation which can swallow the Lawrence myth, could swallow anything."

27. Campbell crossed out "He also fell for the gyppo's nighty, as Canning fell for the Spanish . . . in Hookham Frere."

28. Campbell crossed out "(many critics have speculated)."

29. Campbell crossed out "isolated."

30. Campbell crossed out "Sherlock Holmes."

31. Campbell crossed out the lines:

> To wake up to steeper quays than Europe's,
> To see mysterious ports in the solitude of the Ocean,
> To double distant capes and burst on sudden view
> Landscapes of innumerable, startled coasts.

32. Campbell crossed out "queerest."

33. Campbell crossed out the beginning of a new sentence: "He says of the coast of the Indian ocean."

34. Campbell crossed out "gloomy."

35. Printed here from elsewhere in Campbell's notebooks is the longer of his two attempts to translate stanzas 1 and 3 of "O Mostrengo," the poem Campbell called "the greatest sea-lyric ever written" ("Olive Schreiner").

Works Cited

Alberto de Lacerda: O mundo de um poeta. Lisbon: Fundação Calouste Gulbenkian/Centro de Arte Moderna, 1987.

Alexander, Peter. *Roy Campbell: A Critical Biography*. Oxford: Oxford Univ. Press, 1982.

————. *William Plomer: A Biography*. Oxford: Oxford Univ. Press, 1989.

Almeida, Onésimo Teotónio. *Mensagem: Uma tentativa de reinterpretação*. Angra do Heroísmo: Secretaria Regional da Educação e Cultura, 1987.

————. "Sobre a mundividência Zen de Pessoa-Caeiro (O interesse de Thomas Merton e D.T. Suzuki)." *Nova Renascença* 6 (Spring 1986), 146-52.

Bell, Aubrey F.G., ed. *Oxford Book of Portuguese Verse*. Oxford: Clarendon Press, 1925.

Blanco, José. "Álvaro de Campos Insone." In *De Baudelaire a Lorca*. Kassel: Edition Reichenberger, 1996.

————. *Fernando Pessoa: esboço de uma bibliografia*. Lisbon: Imprensa Nacional-Casa da Moeda/Centro de Estudos Pessoanos, 1983.

Bloom, Harold. *The Western Canon: The Books and School of the Ages*. New York: Harcourt Brace, 1994.

Brodsky, Joseph. "How to Read a Book." *New York Times Book Review*, June 12, 1988, p. 29.

Brown, Susan, Epstein, Thomas, and Henry Gould, eds. *A Glass of Green Tea— With Honig*. Providence, R.I.: Alephoe Books, 1994.

Burnshaw, Stanley, ed. *The Poem Itself*. New York: Holt, Rinehart and Winston, 1960.

Campbell, Roy. *Adamastor*. London: Faber & Faber, 1930.

————. *Collected Works I-IV*. Edited by Peter F. Alexander, Michael Chapman, and Marcia Leveson. Craighall, S.A.: Ad. Donker, 1985-88.

————. *Light on a Dark Horse: An Autobiography, 1901-1935*. London: Hollis & Carter, 1951.

————. "Olive Schreiner: Crusading without a Cross." Manuscript. Harry Ransom Humanities Research Center, Univ. of Texas at Austin.

————. Papers. Harry Ransom Humanities Research Center, Univ. of Texas at Austin.

————. *Portugal*. Chicago: Henry Regnery, 1958.

————. *Selected Poetry*. Edited by Joseph M. Lalley. Chicago: Henry Regnery, 1968.

————. *Talking Bronco*. London: Faber & Faber, 1946.

———. "Translator's Note." In *Poems of Baudelaire: A Translation of "Les fleurs du mal,"* trans. Roy Campbell. New York: Pantheon, 1952.

Deutsch, Babette. "American and British Verse." *New Freeman* 3 (April 15, 1931), 117.

Downes, Leonard S. *Portuguese Poems and Translations.* Lisbon: n.p., 1947.

Eglington, Charles. "Homage to Fernando Pessoa." *Contrast 16,* 4:4. (June 1967), 16-19.

———. *Under the Horizon: Collected Poems of Charles Eglington.* Edited by Jack Cope. Cape Town: Purnell, 1977.

Ellmann, Richard. *Yeats: The Man and the Masks.* New York: W.W. Norton, 1978.

Epstein, Thomas. "On the Usefulness of Dinosaurs or *le cas* Edouard Roditi." *Alea* 3 (Fall 1933), 132-45.

Ferlinghetti, Lawrence. *A Coney Island of the Mind.* New York: New Directions, 1958.

———. *Love in the Days of Rage.* New York: E.P. Dutton, 1988.

Ferreira e Sousa, Rui. "Lawrence Ferlinghetti: 'Vivemos na era dos robotechs.'" *Jornal de Letras* 6 (July 28 to Aug. 3, 1986), p. 7.

Folsom, Ed. "Talking Back to Walt Whitman: An Introduction." In *Walt Whitman: The Measure of His Song,* ed. Jim Perlman, Ed Folsom, and Dan Campion. Minneapolis: Holy Cow! Press, 1981.

Ginsberg, Allen. "Allen Ginsberg on Walt Whitman: Composed on the Tongue." In *Walt Whitman: The Measure of His Song,* ed. Jim Perlman, Ed Folsom, and Dan Campion. Minneapolis: Holy Cow! Press, 1981.

———. *Collected Poems, 1947-1980.* New York: Harper & Row, 1984.

———. *Cosmopolitan Greetings: Poems, 1986-1992.* New York: Harper Collins, 1994.

———. *White Shroud: Poems, 1980-1985.* New York: Harper & Row, 1986.

Gray, Stephen, ed. *Penguin Book of Southern African Verse.* London: Penguin Group, 1989.

———. *Southern African Literature: An Introduction.* New York: Barnes & Noble, 1979.

Hamburger, Michael. *Collected Poems, 1941-1983.* Manchester: Carcanet, 1984.

———. *A Mug's Game: Intermittent Memoirs, 1924-1954.* Cheadel, Cheshire: Carcanet, 1973.

———. *Testimonies: Selected Shorter Prose, 1950-1987.* New York: St. Martin's Press, 1989.

———. *The Truth of Poetry: Tensions in Modern Poetry from Baudelaire to the 1960s.* New York: Harcourt, Brace & World, 1969.

Harvey, Andrew, trans. "Fernando Pessoa." *Normal* 3 (Winter 1987), 16-23.

———. *No Diamonds, No Hat, No Honey.* Boston: Houghton Mifflin, 1985.

Hollander, John. "Quadrophenia." *New Republic,* Sept. 7, 1987, pp. 33-36.

Honig, Edwin. Comment in "Encerrou na Gulbenkian a Babel da Ilha Pessoana." In *Um século de Pessoa: Encontro internacional do centenário de Fernando Pessoa,* ed. Isabel Tamen. Lisbon: Secretaria de Estado da Cultura, 1990. (Originally published in *Europeu,* Dec. 8, 1988.)

————. *Dark Conceit: The Making of Allegory.* Hanover, N.H.: Brown Univ. Press, Univ. Press of New England, 1982.

————. "Fernando Pessoa: A Translator's View." In *Um século de Pessoa: Encontro internacional do centenário de Fernando Pessoa,* ed. Isabel Tamen. Lisbon: Secretaria de Estado da Cultura, 1990.

————. *Gifts of Light.* Isla Vista, Calif.: Turkey Press, 1983. (*Dádivas de luz,* trans. António Ramos Rosa [Lisbon: Caminho, 1992.])

————. *The Imminence of Love: Poems, 1962-1992.* Montrose, Ala.: Texas Center for Writer's Press, 1993.

————. *Interrupted Praise: New and Selected Poems.* Metuchen, N.J.: Scarecrow Press, 1983.

————. "Introduction." In *The Poet's Other Voice: Conversations on Literary Translation.* Amherst: Univ. of Massachusetts Press, 1985.

————. "Introduction: Some Words in the Entryway." In *Always Astonished: Selected Prose.* Translated by Edwin Honig. San Francisco: City Lights Books, 1988.

————. "An Open Reply to August Willemsen, Author of 'Fernando Pessoa as American Heteronym.'" *Persona* 7 (Aug. 1982), 52.

————. "Preface: A Note on the Translations." In *Selected Poems by Fernando Pessoa.* Translated by Edwin Honig. Chicago: Swallow, 1971.

————. "Translator's Note." In *ND: New Directions in Poetry and Prose 23.* New York: New Directions, 1971.

Jennings, Hubert D. "Eglington—Thorny Path of Perfection." *Contrast 49,* 13:1 (June 1980), 84-89.

————. "The Many Faces of Pessoa." *Contrast 27,* 7:3 (Nov. 1971), 51-64.

Johnson, Greg. *Joyce Carol Oates: A Study of the Short Fiction.* New York: Twayne, 1994.

K. "Fernando Pessoa: O mito e a realidade." In *O banquiero anarquista.* Lisbon: Antígona, 1981.

Leckey, Hugo. "Borges for Breakfast." In *A Glass of Green Tea—With Honig,* ed. Susan Brown, Thomas Epstein, and Henry Gould. Providence, R.I.: Alephoe Books, 1994.

Lisboa, Eugénio. "'Homenagem a Fernando Pessoa' por um poeta de língua inglesa: Charles Eglington." In *As vinte e cinco notas do texto.* Lisbon: Imprensa Nacional-Casa da Moeda, 1987.

Lisboa, Eugénio, and L.C. Taylor, eds. *A Centenary Pessoa.* Manchester: Carcarnet, 1995.

L[ivermore], H[arold] V. Review of Roy Campbell's translation of "O primo Basílio." *Atlante* 2:1 (1954), 48-49.

Lopes, Teresa Rita, ed. *II: Pessoa por conhecer: Textos para um novo mapa.* Lisbon: Estampa, 1990.

————, ed. *Pessoa inédito.* Lisbon: Livros Horizonte, 1993.

Matos, Carolina. "Edwin Honig and Jean Longland: Two Interviews." In *The Man Who Never Was: Essays on Fernando Pessoa,* ed. George Monteiro. Providence, R.I.: Gávea-Brown, 1982.

Merton, Thomas. *Cables to the Ace,* In *The Collected Poems of Thomas Merton.* New York: New Directions, 1977.

————. *The Collected Poems of Thomas Merton.* New York: New Directions, 1977.

————. *The Courage for Truth: The Letters of Thomas Merton to Writers.* Edited by Christine M. Bochen. New York: Farrar, Straus & Giroux, 1993.

————. "Day of a Stranger." *Hudson Review* 20 (Summer 1967), 211-18.

————. "From the Portuguese of Fernando Pessoa: Twelve Poems from *The Keeper of the Flocks.*" In *The Collected Poems of Thomas Merton.* New York: New Directions, 1977.

————. *The Hidden Ground of Love: The Letters of Thomas Merton on Religious Experience and Social Concerns.* Edited by William H. Shannon. New York: Farrar, Straus & Giroux, 1985.

————. *The School of Charity: The Letters of Thomas Merton on Religious Renewal and Spiritual Direction.* Edited by Brother Patrick Hart. New York: Farrar, Straus & Giroux, 1990.

————. "Translator's Note." In *The Literary Essays of Thomas Merton,* ed. Brother Patrick Hart. New York: New Directions, 1981.

————. *A Vow of Conversation: Journals 1964-1965.* Edited by Naomi Burton Stone. New York: Farrar, Straus & Giroux, 1988.

————. *Zen and the Birds of Appetite.* New York: New Directions, 1968.

Monteiro, Adolfo Casais. *A poesia de Fernando Pessoa.* 2d ed. Edited by José Blanco. Lisbon: Imprensa Nacional-Casa da Moeda, 1985.

Monteiro, George. "Jorge de Sena/Edith Sitwell: Correspondence." *Santa Barbara Portuguese Studies* 1 (1994), 5-28.

————, ed. *The Man Who Never Was: Essays on Fernando Pessoa.* Providence, R.I.: Gávea-Brown, 1982.

"Notes." *Contrast* 16, 4:4 (June 1967), 94.

Oates, Joyce Carol. "Does the Writer Exist?" In *(Woman) Writer: Occasions and Opportunities.* New York: E.P. Dutton, 1988.

————. *"The Poisoned Kiss" and Other Stories from the Portuguese.* New York: Vanguard, 1975.

————. "Pseudonymous Selves." In *(Woman) Writer: Occasions and Opportunities.* New York: E.P. Dutton, 1988.

————. *(Woman) Writer: Occasions and Opportunities.* New York: E.P. Dutton, 1988.

Orpheu 1. 4th ed. Lisbon: Ática, 1984.

Paton, Alan. Review of Rowland Smith's *Lyric and Polemic: The Literary Personality of Roy Campbell. Research in African Literatures* 6 (Spring 1975), 120-25.

Paz, Octavio. *Cuadrivio.* Barcelona: Biblioteca de Bolsillo, 1991.

————. "El desconocido de sí mismo." In *Cuadrivio.* Barcelona: Biblioteca de Bolsillo, 1991. ("Introduction: Pessoa; or, The Imminence of the Unknown," in *Selected Poems by Fernando Pessoa,* trans. Edwin Honig [Chicago: Swallow, 1971].)

Perlman, Jim, Ed Folsom, and Dan Campion, eds. *Walt Whitman: The Measure of His Song.* Minneapolis: Holy Cow! Press, 1981.

Pessoa, Fernando. *Always Astonished: Selected Prose.* Translated by Edwin Honig. San Francisco: City Lights Books, 1988.

————. "The Anarchist Banker: A Fiction." In *Always Astonished: Selected Prose,* trans. by Edwin Honig. San Francisco: City Lights Books, 1988.

————. "Autopsicografia," *Presença* 36 (Nov. 1932), 9.

————. *O banqueiro anarquista.* Lisbon: Antígona, 1981.

————. "English Poems." *Literary Review* 6 (Spring 1963), 385-91.

————. "Maritime Ode." Translated by Edwin Honig. In *ND: New Directions in Prose and Poetry 23,* ed. J. Laughlin. New York: New Directions, 1971.

————. *Obra poética.* Edited by Maria Aliete Galhoz. Rio de Janeiro: Aguilar, 1960.

————. *Páginas íntimas e de auto-interpretação.* Edited by Georg Rudolf Lind and Jacinto do Prado Coelho. Lisbon: Ática, 1966.

————. "Poema." Translated by Charles David Ley. *Presença* 3:53-54 (Nov. 1938), 11.

————. *Poemas de Álvaro de Campos.* Edited by Cleonice Berardinelli. *Edição crítica de Fernando Pessoa, vol. 2.* Lisbon: Imprensa Nacional-Casa da Moeda, 1990.

————. *Poemas ingleses, vol. 1: Antinous, Inscriptions, Epithalamium, 35 Sonnets.* Edited by João Dionísio. Lisbon: Imprensa Nacional-Casa da Moeda, 1993.

————. *Poems of Fernando Pessoa.* Translated by Edwin Honig and Susan M. Brown. New York: Ecco Press, 1986.

————. *Selected Poems.* Translated by Peter Rickard. Austin: Univ. of Texas Press, 1971.

————. *Selected Poems.* 2d ed., supplemented. Translated by Jonathan Griffin. Harmondsworth: Penguin Books, 1982.

————. *Selected Poems by Fernando Pessoa.* Translated by Edwin Honig. Chicago: Swallow, 1971.

————. *Self-Analysis and Thirty Other Poems.* Translated by George Monteiro. Lisbon: Calouste Gulbenkian Foundation, 1988.

————. "Sieben Gedichte." Translated by Paul Celan and Edouard Roditi. *Die Neue Rundschau* 67:2/3 (1956), 401-10.

————. *Sixty Portuguese Poems.* Translated by F.E.G. Quintanilha. Cardiff: Univ. of Wales Press, 1973.

————. *Textos de crítica e de intervenção.* Lisbon: Ática, 1980.

————. *35 Sonnets.* In *Poemas ingleses,* bilingual ed., ed. and trans. Jorge de Sena et al. Lisbon: Ática, 1974.

"Translations: Fernando Pessoa." Translated by Jean R. Longland. *Poet Lore* 66 (Oct. 1970), 280-92.

————. "Twelve Poems." Translated by Thomas Merton. In *ND: New Directions in Prose and Poetry 19,* ed. James Laughlin. New York: New Directions, 1966.

————. *Ultimatum e páginas de sociologia política.* Compiled by Maria Isabel Rocheta and Maria Paula Morão, introd. Joel Serrão. Lisbon: Ática, 1980.

Poetic Translation: A Panel Discussion at the Twelfth Annual Convention of the American Translators Association in Boston, October 24, 1971. Croton-on-Hudson, N.Y.: American Translators Association, 1972.

Review of Roy Campbell's *Mithraic Emblems. New Verse* 23 (Christmas 1936), 26.

Roditi, Edouard. "Autopsychoanalysis." *World Letter* 4 (1993), 27.

————. "Fernando Pessoa, forasteiro entre os poetas ingleses." *Ocidente* 46 (May 1964), 205-15.

————. "Fernando Pessoa, Outsider Among English Poets." *Literary Review* 6 (Spring 1963), 372-85.

————. "A máscara inglesa de Fernando Pessoa." *Lusíada* 2 (Dec. 1954), 89-93.

————. "Schein und Sein in Leben and Dichtung des Fernando Pessoa." Translated by Francisco Tanzer. *Die Neue Rundschau* 67:2/3 (1956), 395-400.

————. "The Several Names of Fernando Pessoa." *Poetry* 87 (Oct. 1955), 40-44.

————. "The Warning." *World Letter* 4 (1993), 26.

Rodway, Allan. *Poetry of the 1930s.* London: Longmans, 1967.

"Rum Tum Tum on a Broken Drum." *New Verse*, n.s., 1:2 (May 1939), 52, 54.

Schumacher, Michael. "Joyce Carol Oates and the Hardest Part of Writing." In *Conversations with Joyce Carol Oates*, ed. Lee Milazzo. Jackson: Univ. Press of Mississippi, 1989.

Schwerner, Armand. "Old Dog Sermon." In *Poets on Stage: The Some Symposium on Poetry Readings (Some #9).* New York: Release Press, 1978.

Sena, Jorge de. *A literatura inglêsa.* São Paulo: Cultrix, 1963.

————. "Resposta a três perguntas de Luciana Stegagno Picchio Sobre Fernando Pessoa." In *Fernando Pessoa & CaHeterónima.* Lisbon: Edições 70, 1982.

Sena, Mécia de, ed. *Eduardo Lourenço/Jorge de Sena correspondência.* Lisbon: Imprensa Nacional-Casa da Moeda, 1991.

Shange, Ntozake. "Spell #7." In *Three Pieces.* New York: St. Martin's Press, 1981.

Shannon, William H. *Thomas Merton's Dark Path.* New York: Farrar, Straus & Giroux, 1981.

Shapiro, Karl. "On First Looking into Honig's Pessoa." In Fernando Pessoa, *The Keeper of Sheep*, trans. Edwin Honig and Susan M. Brown. Riverdale-on-Hudson, N.Y.; Sheep Meadow Press, 1986.

Silesky, Barry. *Ferlinghetti: The Artist in His Time.* New York: Warner Books, 1990.

Silk, Dennis. *The Punished Land.* New York: Viking, 1980.

Simões, João Gaspar. *Fernando Pessoa: Breve história da sua vida e da sua obra.* Lisbon: Difel, 1983.

————. *Fernando Pessoa, Escorço interpretativo da sua vida e obra.* Cadernos Culturais Inquérito 91. Lisbon: Inquérito, 1963.

————. "Uma explicação da vida e da obra de Fernando Pessoa." In *Heteropsicografia de Fernando Pessoa.* Porto: Inova, 1973.

Skelton, Robin, ed. *Poetry of the Thirties.* Harmondsworth: Penguin Books, 1964.

Smith, Rowland. Review. *Research in African Literatures* 15 (Spring 1984), 140-47.

Steiner, George. "Foursome: The Art of Fernando Pessoa." *New Yorker,* Jan. 8, 1996, pp. 76-80.

Tamen, Isabel, ed. *Um século de Pessoa: Encontro internacional do centenário de Fernando Pessoa.* Lisbon: Secretaria de Estado da Cultura, 1990.

van Innis, Benoit. Spot drawings. *New Yorker,* June 21, 1993, p. 62; April 3, 1995, p. 44; and June 26 & July 3, 1995, p. 66.

Vidigal, B. "Note to Second Edition." In *The Oxford Book of Portuguese Verse,* ed. Aubrey F.G. Bell. 2d ed., ed. B. Vidigal. Oxford: Clarendon Press, 1952.

Wain, John. *Poems, 1949-1979.* London: Macmillan, 1980.

———. *The Free Zone Stops Here.* New York: Delacorte, 1982.

———. "Glare and Shadow." *Spectator,* March 4, 1960, pp. 326, 328.

———. *Reflexões sobre o Sr. Pessoa.* Translated by João Almeida Flor, with a note by Joaquim Manuel Magalhães. Coimbra: Fenda, 1981; reprint, Lisbon: Cotovia, 1993.

———. "A Salute to the Makers." *Encounter* 35 (Nov. 1970), 51-59.

———. "Thinking About Mr. Person." *New Lugano Review* 2 (Oct.-Dec. 1979), 73-77.

———. *Thinking About Mr Person With Two Etchings by Bartolomeu dos Santos.* Kent: Chimaera Press, 1980.

White, Edmund. "The Hearts of Men." *Vogue,* Jan. 1987, pp. 94, 96.

White, Edmund, and Edouard Roditi. "Conversation on an Island in the Seine." *Conjunctions* 7 (1985), 143-56.

Index